TEACHER RECOMMENDED

2ND GRADE
COMMON CORE
MATH

DAILY PRACTICE BOOK

ARGOPREP.COM

FREE ONLINE SYSTEM WITH VIDEO EXPLANATIONS

ArgoPrep is one of the leading providers of supplemental educational products and services. We offer affordable and effective test prep solutions to educators, parents and students. Learning should be fun and easy! For that reason, most of our workbooks come with detailed video answer explanations taught by one of our fabulous instructors.

Our goal is to make your life easier, so let us know how we can help you by e-mailing us at:
info@argoprep.com.

ISBN: 9781951048655
Published by Argo Brothers, Inc.

Aknowlegments:
Icons made by Freepik, Creaticca Creative Agency, Pixel perfect , Pixel Buddha, Smashicons, Twitter , Good Ware, Smalllikeart, Nikita Golubev, monkik, DinosoftLabs, Icon Pond from www.flaticon.com

Our Awards

- ArgoPrep is a recipient of the prestigious **Mom's Choice Award.**

- ArgoPrep also received the 2019 **Seal of Approval** from Homeschool.com for our award-winning workbooks.

- ArgoPrep was awarded the 2019 **National Parenting Products Award, Gold Medal Parent's Choice Award** and **the Tillywig Brain Child Award.**

TABLE OF CONTENTS

HOW TO USE THE BOOK

This workbook is designed to give lots of practice with the math Common Core State Standards (CCSS). By practicing and mastering this entire workbook, your child will become very familiar and comfortable with the state math exam. If you are a teacher using this workbook for your students, you will notice each question is labeled with the specific standard so you can easily assign your students problems in the workbook. This workbook takes the CCSS and divides them up among 20 weeks. By working on these problems on a daily basis, students will be able to (1) find any deficiencies in their understanding and/or practice of math and (2) have small successes each day that will build proficiency and confidence in their abilities.

We strongly recommend watching the videos as they will reinforce the fundamental concepts. Please note, scrap paper may be necessary while using this workbook so that the student has sufficient space to show their work.

For a detailed overview of the Common Core State Standards for 2nd grade, please visit: www.corestandards.org/Math/Content/2/introduction/

How to access video explantions?

Download our app: **ArgoPrep Video Explanations** to access videos on any mobile device or tablet.

You also can access it on our website:

Step 1 - Visit our website at: www.argoprep.com/k8

Step 2 - Click on the Video Explanations button located on the top right corner.

Step 3 - Choose the workbook you have and enjoy video explanations.

OTHER BOOKS BY ARGOPREP

Here are some other test prep workbooks by ArgoPrep you may be interested in. All of our workbooks come equipped with detailed video explanations to make your learning experience a breeze! Visit us at **www.argoprep.com**

COMMON CORE MATH SERIES

    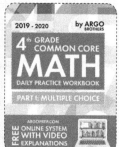

COMMON CORE ELA SERIES

  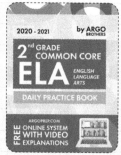  

INTRODUCING MATH!

Introducing Math! by ArgoPrep is an award-winning series created by certified teachers to provide students with high-quality practice problems. Our workbooks include topic overviews with instruction, practice questions, answer explanations along with digital access to video explanations. Practice in confidence - with ArgoPrep!

   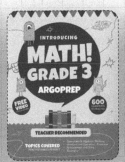 

SCIENCE SERIES

Science Daily Practice Workbook by ArgoPrep is an award-winning series created by certified science teachers to help build mastery of foundational science skills. Our workbooks explore science topics in depth with ArgoPrep s 5 E S to build science mastery.

KIDS SUMMER ACADEMY SERIES

ArgoPrep's **Kids Summer Academy** series helps prevent summer learning loss and gets students ready for their new school year by reinforcing core foundations in math, english and science. Our workbooks also introduce new concepts so students can get a head start and be on top of their game for the new school year!

SUMMER ACTIVITY PLAYGROUND SERIES

Summer Activity Playground is another summer series that is designed to prevent summer learning loss and prepares students for the new school year. Students will be able to practice math, ELA, science, social studies and more! This is a new released series that offers the latest aligned learning standards for each grade.

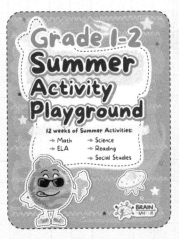
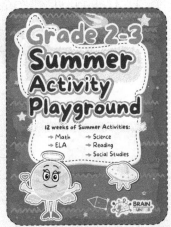

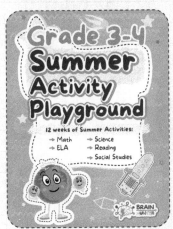
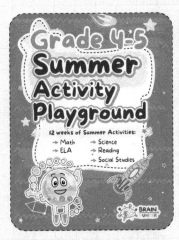

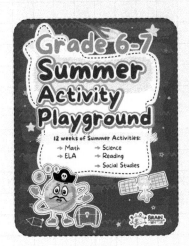

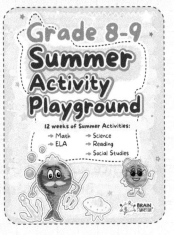

For more practice with 2nd Grade Math, be sure to check out our other book, Argo Brothers Math Workbook Grade: Free Response

WEEK 1

VIDEO
EXPLANATIONS

ARGOPREP.COM

This week we are reading and writing numbers using standard form, word form and expanded form. The numbers will go up to 3 digit numbers.

You can find detailed video explanations of each problem in the book by visiting:
ArgoPrep.com

WEEK I : DAY I

1. Which number is shown using the base ten pieces? **(Look at Diagram 1 below).**

   A. 460
   B. 469
   C. 690
   D. 964

   2.NBT.3

2. Which shows the number of hundreds in the number 618?

   A. 0
   B. 1
   C. 6
   D. 8

   2.NBT.1

3. In which place is the digit 3 in the number 439?

   A. Ones
   B. Tens
   C. Hundreds
   D. Thousands

   2.NBT.1

4. Which number is made up of 5 tens, 8 ones and 2 hundreds?

   A. 258
   B. 285
   C. 582
   D. 528

   2.NBT.1

5. Which model shows the number 204?

   A.
   B.
   C.
   D.

   2.NBT.3

We use the digits 0-1-2-3-4-5-6-7-8-9 to form numbers.
The value of the digit is based on the place that the digit is in.
For example: 2 in the *ones* place has a value of *2*
2 in the *tens* place has a value of *20*
2 in the *hundreds* place has a value of *200*

of the

Diagram 1

| Hundreds Place | Tens Place | Ones Place |

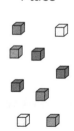

1. Which shows another way to write the number 100?

   A. One one
   B. One ten
   C. Ten tens
   D. Ten hundreds

2.NBT.1a

2. Which number is made up of 8 hundreds and 7 tens?

   A. 78
   B. 87
   C. 807
   D. 870

2.NBT.1

3. Which number is made up of 6 ones and 3 tens?

   A. 36
   B. 63
   C. 306
   D. 603

2.NBT.1

4. Which statement is true about the number 500?

   A. It is made up of 5 ones
   B. It is made up of 5 tens and 0 ones
   C. It is made up of 5 hundreds, 5 tens and 0 ones
   D. It is made up of 5 hundreds, 0 tens and 0 ones

2.NBT.1b

5. In the number 902, which place has no value?

   A. Ones
   B. Tens
   C. Hundreds
   D. Thousands

2.NBT.1

6. The model below shows which two values?

Hundreds	Tens	Ones
		■ ■
		■ ■
		■ ■
		■ ■
		■ ■

   A. Ten ones or One ten
   B. Ten tens or One one
   C. One hundred or Ten ones
   D. One hundred or Ten tens

2.NBT.1a

TIP *of the* **DAY**

When we have a total of 10 of one place, it is equal to 1 of the place to the left.

10 ones = 1 ten

When we have no value in a place, we use the digit 0.
105 = 1 hundred, 0 tens, 5 ones

13

WEEK 1 : DAY 3

1. Which shows the written form of the number 415?

A. Forty-one
B. Forty- fifteen
C. Four hundred fifteen
D. Four hundred fifty-one

2.NBT.3

2. Which shows the expanded form of 7 hundreds and 6 tens?

A. 70 + 6
B. 70 + 60
C. 700 + 6
D. 700 + 60

2.NBT.1 & 3

3. Which shows the standard form of the number eight hundred thirty-seven?

A. 37
B. 830
C. 837
D. 8307

2.NBT.3

4. Which shows the written form of 900 + 20 + 9?

A. Ninety-nine
B. Ninety twenty-nine
C. Nine hundred nine
D. Nine hundred twenty-nine

2.NBT.3

5. Which shows the expanded form of the diagram shown below?

A. 100 + 70 + 4
B. 100 + 70 + 40
C. 400 + 70 + 1
D. 700 + 40 + 1

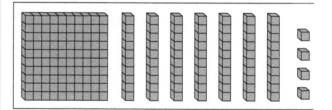

2.NBT.3

TIP of the DAY

Numbers can be written in standard form, written form and expanded form.

Standard Form	Written Form	Expanded Form
123	One hundred twenty-three	100 + 20 + 3

1. Start at 200 and skip-count by 100. Which would be the first 5 numbers?

   A. 100, 110, 120, 130, 140,
   B. 100, 200, 300, 400, 500
   C. 200, 210, 220, 230, 240
   D. 200, 300, 400, 500, 600

   2.NBT.2

2. Start at 30 and skip-count by 5. Which would be the first 5 numbers?

   A. 5, 10, 15, 20, 25
   B. 30, 35, 40, 45, 50
   C. 30, 40, 50, 60, 70
   D. 40. 45, 50, 55, 60

   2.NBT.2

3. Ana's number pattern is shown:
   180, 190, 200, 210, 220

   Ana is skip-counting by which number in her number pattern?

   A. 1
   B. 5
   C. 10
   D. 100

   2.NBT.2

4. Start at the number shown below by the model and skip-count by 5. Which shows the first 5 numbers?

   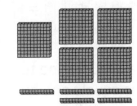

   A. 55, 60, 65, 70, 75
   B. 55, 65, 75, 85, 95
   C. 550, 555, 560, 565, 570
   D. 500, 600, 700, 800, 900

   2.NBT.2 & 3

5. Start at the number shown: **4 hundreds, 0 tens, 0 ones**. Skip count by 100. Which shows the first 5 numbers?

   A. 400, 401, 402, 403, 404
   B. 405, 410, 415, 420, 425
   C. 410, 420, 430, 440, 450
   D. 400, 500, 600, 700, 800

   2.NBT.1 & 2

6. A number pattern is shown:
   70 ___ 90 ___ ___ 120
   Which shows the missing numbers?

   A. 71, 91, 101
   B. 75, 95, 105
   C. 80, 100, 110
   D. 85, 95, 100

   2.NBT.2

TIP of the DAY

When skip-counting by a given number, just keep adding the same number. Example: Counting by 10s from the number 30.   30, 40, 50, 60...

WEEK 1 : DAY 5

1. Which can be shown by the model?

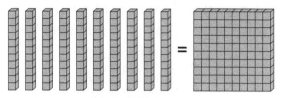

   A. Ten ones equals one ten
   B. Ten tens equals one hundred
   C. Ten ones equals one hundred
   D. Ten hundreds equals one ten   2.NBT.1a

2. Which shows the written form of the number shown in the chart?

H	T	O
1	7	0

   A. One hundred seven
   B. One hundred seventeen
   C. One hundred seventy
   D. One hundred seventy-seven   2.NBT.3

3. Which shows the standard form of the number shown? **5 tens 0 hundreds 6 ones**

   A. 56
   B. 65
   C. 506
   D. 650

                                         2.NBT.1
                                         2.NBT.3

4. Which shows the expanded form of the number shown by the model?

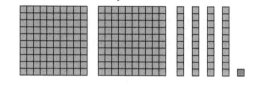

   A. 20 + 4   C. 200 + 4
   B. 20 + 40 + 1   D. 200 + 40 + 1
                                         2.NBT.3

5. Max made the number pattern shown:
   390 ____ 410 420 430

   Which shows the number that Max skip-counted by and the missing number?

   A. Skip-counted by 10, Missing number = 400
   B. Skip-counted by 10, Missing number = 440
   C. Skip-counted by 100, Missing number = 400
   D. Skip-counted by 100, Missing number = 500   2.NBT.2

6. Which shows another way to write the number 890?

   A. 8 tens and 9 ones
   B. 8 tens and 90 ones
   C. 8 hundreds, 0 tens, 9 ones
   D. 8 hundreds, 9 tens and 0 ones   2.NBT.1

DAY 6
Challenge question

Ella wrote a number. She used the following clues:
• There is a 7 in the tens place
• There is a 2 in the hundreds place
• There is a 0 in the number
What is the standard form, written form and expanded form of Ella's number?
                                         2.NBT.1 & 2.NBT.3

16

WEEK 2

: VIDEO
EXPLANATIONS ▶

ARGOPREP.COM

This week we are comparing numbers to find which is greater or less than another number. The numbers will go up to 3 digit numbers.

You can find detailed video explanations of each problem in the book by visiting: ArgoPrep.com

WEEK 2 : DAY 1

1. Which number correctly completes the number sentence?

    882 > ?

    A. 891
    B. 980
    C. 890
    D. 879

    2.NBT.4

2. Which number sentence is correct?

    A. 319 < 318
    B. 417 < 409
    C. 324 < 333
    D. 428 < 428

    2.NBT.4

3. Which number is less than the number shown in the model?

    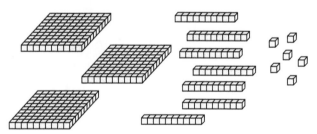

    A. 374
    B. 475
    C. 376
    D. 481

    2.NBT.3
    2.NBT.4

4. Which number sentence is correct?

    A. 500 + 20 + 7 > 519
    B. 506 > 500 + 50
    C. 500 + 9 > 580
    D. 550 > 500 + 60

    2.NBT.3
    2.NBT.4

5. Which number completes the sentence?

    One hundred forty-seven = ?

    A. 100 + 70 + 4
    B. 100 + 40 + 7
    C. 100 + 4 + 17
    D. 100 + 7 + 14

    2.NBT.3
    2.NBT.4

TIP of the DAY

When comparing/ordering numbers in two different forms (standard, word, expanded) re-write them both in standard form before comparing them.

1. Which symbol completes the number sentence?

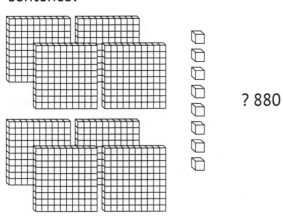 ? 880

- **A.** <
- **B.** >
- **C.** =

2.NBT.3
2.NBT.4

2. Which number completes the number sentence?

3 hundreds, 5 tens, 0 ones < ?

- **A.** 45
- **B.** 36
- **C.** 354
- **D.** 350

2.NBT.3
2.NBT.4

3. Which number completes the number sentence?

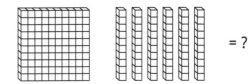 = ?

- **A.** 16
- **B.** 61
- **C.** 106
- **D.** 160

2.NBT.3
2.NBT.4

4. Which symbol completes the number sentence?

Six hundred seven ? 600 + 60

- **A.** <
- **B.** >
- **C.** =

2.NBT.3
2.NBT.4

5. Which number completes the number sentence?

800 + 2 + 70 < ?

- **A.** 849
- **B.** 838
- **C.** 881
- **D.** 870

2.NBT.3
2.NBT.4

TIP of the DAY

When comparing two numbers with the same number of digits, the digit in the largest place should be compared first. If those digits are the same, look to the digit to the right. If they are still the same, continue looking to the next digit to the right to compare.

WEEK 2 : DAY 3

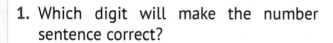

1. Which digit will make the number sentence correct?

$$736 < 7\_2$$

A. 1
B. 2
C. 3
D. 4

2.NBT.4

2. Which digit will make the number sentence correct?

5 tens, 3 hundreds and 4 ones < __55

A. 0
B. 3
C. 2
D. 1

2.NBT.1
2.NBT.4

3. Which digit will make the number sentence correct?

Three hundred seventy > 3 hundreds __ tens 7 ones

A. 7
B. 8
C. 6
D. 9

2.NBT.1
2.NBT.4

4. The table shows the number of shirts in 4 different colors at a store.

Shirt Color	Red	Blue	Green	Yellow
Number of Shirts	104	121	112	103

When comparing the number of shirts, which sentence is correct?

A. Red shirts < Green shirts
B. Blue shirts < Yellow shirts
C. Green shirts < Red shirts
D. Red shirts < Yellow shirts

2.NBT.4

5. The table shows the number of children in grades 1, 2 and 3.

Grade	1	2	3
Number of Children	179	161	?

The number of children in grade 1 is greater than the number of children in grade 3.
The number of children in grade 3 is greater than the number of children in grade 2.

Which number could be the number of children in grade 3?

A. 165   C. 180
B. 156   D. 161

2.NBT.4

TIP of the DAY

When comparing numbers with missing digits, place the answer choices in the blanks to find the answer.

WEEK 2 : DAY 4

1. Which symbol completes the number sentence?

4 hundreds and 11 tens ? 510

A. <
B. >
C. =

2.NBT.1
2.NBT.4

2. Which number completes the number sentence?

8 hundreds, 2 tens, 14 ones < ?

A. 824
B. 814
C. 833
D. 835

2.NBT.1
2.NBT.4

3. Which digit makes the number sentence correct?

5 hundreds, 7 tens, 16 ones = 5?6

A. 6
B. 7
C. 8
D. 9

2.NBT.1
2.NBT.4

4. Which number makes the number sentence correct?

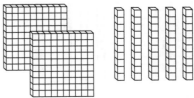

= ?

A. 215
B. 250
C. 255
D. 265

2.NBT.3
2.NBT.3

5. Which number sentence is not correct?

A. 715 < 7 hundreds 1 ten 15 ones
B. 517 < 4 hundreds 11 tens 8 ones
C. 618 < 5 hundreds 11 tens 8 ones
D. 816 < 8 hundreds 1 ten 16 ones

2.NBT.1 & 4

6. Which symbol makes the number sentence correct?

A. <
B. >
C. =

? 8 hundreds 4 tens 12 ones

2.NBT.3 & 2.NBT

TIP of the DAY

Numbers can be written in more than one way.
For example: 82 can be written as 8 tens and 2 ones or 7 tens and 12 ones.
340 can be written as 3 hundreds and 4 tens or 2 hundreds and 14 tens.
When comparing numbers, be sure to use the standard form of both numbers.

21

WEEK 2 : DAY 5

1. Which number completes the number sentence?

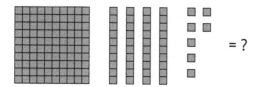

= ?

A. 145
B. 147
C. 174
D. 177

2.NBT.3
2.NBT.4

2. Which symbol completes the number sentence?

4 hundreds 6 tens 11 ones ? 461

A. <
B. >
C. =

2.NBT.1
2.NBT.4

3. Which digit completes the number sentence?

Nine hundred seventy-two > 9 hundreds __ tens 4 ones

A. 9
B. 6
C. 7
D. 8

2.NBT.1
2.NBT.4

4. The number of flowers in the garden is less than 415 and greater than 409.

Which could be the number of flowers in the garden?

A. 416
B. 406
C. 415
D. 411

2.NBT.4

5. Which number sentence is correct?

A. 6 hundreds 12 tens = 612
B. 7 hundreds 7 tens < 717
C. 6 hundreds 8 ones > 680
D. 7 hundreds 11 tens > 711

2.NBT.1
2.NBT.4

6. Which number completes the number sentence?

2 hundreds 6 ones 1 ten > ?

A. 250
B. 215
C. 260
D. 216

2.NBT.1
2.NBT.4

DAY 6
Challenge question

Part A: Find the mystery number using the clues:
There are 3 hundreds. There are 12 tens. There are 12 ones.
Mystery Number: ___ ___ ___
Part B: Compare the mystery number to the number shown by circling the correct symbol:
Mystery Number < 322, ? > ?, ? = ?

2.NBT.1

22

WEEK 3

VIDEO EXPLANATIONS ▶ ARGOPREP.COM

This week we are adding single digit numbers. The numbers will go up to 9 + 9.

You can find detailed video explanations of each problem in the book by visiting:
ArgoPrep.com

1. Which number completes the number sentence?

$$5 + 2 = ?$$

A. 6
B. 7
C. 8
D. 10

2.OA.2

2. Which number is the sum of 8 and 4?

A. 4
B. 10
C. 12
D. 13

2.OA.2

3. Which number sentence is shown on the number line?

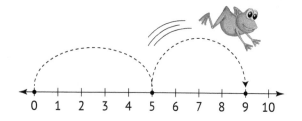

A. $5 + 3 = 8$
B. $5 + 4 = 9$
C. $5 + 5 = 10$
D. $5 + 6 = 11$

2.OA.2

4. The model shows which number sentence?

A. $3 + 0 = 3$
B. $3 + 3 = 6$
C. $4 + 2 = 6$
D. $3 + 4 = 7$

2.OA.2

5. Which number is the sum of 9 and 0?

A. 0
B. 8
C. 9
D. 10

2.OA.2

6. The number 12 is the sum of which number pair?

A. $7 + 5$
B. $6 + 7$
C. $11 + 0$
D. $12 + 1$

2.OA.2

TIP *of the* DAY

The answer to an addition problem is called the "sum". For example, the sum of 3 + 2 is 5.
3 + 2 = 5

24

1. Which number completes the number sentence?

   $$8 + 3 = ?$$

   A. 5   **C.** 11
   B. 10   **D.** 12

   2.OA.2

2. Which number sentence is shown on the number line?

   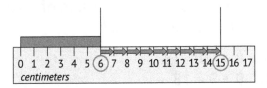

   A. 6 + 6 = 12
   B. 6 + 9 = 15
   C. 0 + 15 = 15
   D. 9 + 9 = 18

   2.OA.2

3. Which pair of number sentences has a sum of 10?

   A. 3 + 7 and 7 + 3
   B. 2 + 7 and 7 + 2
   C. 9 + 0 and 0 + 9
   D. 10 + 1 and 1 + 10

   2.OA.2

4. The model shows which number sentence/pair of number sentences?

6	2

   A. 6 + 0 = 6; 0 + 6 = 6
   B. 6 + 2 = 8; 2 + 6 = 8
   C. 8 + 2 = 10; 2 + 8 = 10
   D. 6 + 6 = 12

   2.OA.2

5. Which number completes the number sentence?

   $$6 + 5 = ?$$

   A. 1
   B. 10
   C. 11
   D. 12

   2.OA.2

6. Which number is the sum of 9 + 2?

   A. 10
   B. 11
   C. 12
   D. 13

   2.OA.2

TIP of the DAY

When adding two numbers, you can change the order and still get the same answer. For example, 4 + 1 = 1 + 4.

25

WEEK 3 : DAY 3

1. The model shows which number sentence?

   A. 2 + 2 = 4   **C.** 4 + 2 = 6
   B. 4 + 0 = 4   **D.** 4 + 4 = 8

2.OA.4

2. Which number sentence can be solved from the model?

   A. 6 + 6 = 12   **C.** 7 + 7 = 14
   B. 6 + 7 = 13   **D.** 7 + 8 = 15

2.OA.1 & 4

3. The model shows which number sentence?

   A. 7 + 2 = 9   **C.** 7 + 7 = 14
   B. 6 + 7 = 13   **D.** 7 + 8 = 15

2.OA.4

4. Which number pair has a sum of 15 and uses a double + 1 to solve?

   A. 7 + 8 = 15
   B. 9 + 6 = 15
   C. 10 + 5 = 15
   D. 14 + 1 = 15

2.OA.1

5. Which number pair has a sum of 18 and uses a double to solve?

   A. 8 + 10 = 18
   B. 9 + 9 = 18
   C. 16 + 2 = 18
   D. 18 + 0 = 18

2.OA.2

6. Which number is the sum of 10 and 10?

   A. 0
   B. 10
   C. 11
   D. 20

2.OA.2

TIP of the DAY

Practice your doubles like 5 + 5 and 6 + 6. Then practice adding 1 on to a double to find the sum. For example: 5 + 5 = 10 and 5 + 6 = 11 which is 10 + 1 more.

1. Which number completes the number sentence?

$$9 + 4 = ?$$

A. 12   C. 14
B. 13   D. 15

2.OA.2

2. Which shows another way to add 8 + 6?

A. 8 + 4   C. 10 + 4
B. 9 + 4   D. 11 + 4

2.OA.2

3. Which pair of number sentences does the model show?

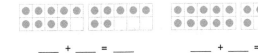

___ + ___ = ___   ___ + ___ = ___

A. 9 + 7 and 10 + 6
B. 9 + 7 and 10 + 7
C. 9 + 6 and 10 + 7
D. 9 + 6 and 10 + 6

2.OA.2

4. Which pair of numbers shows two ways to find the sum of 17?

A. 8 + 7 and 10 + 7
B. 8 + 8 and 10 + 7
C. 9 + 8 and 10 + 7
D. 9 + 9 and 10 + 7

2.OA.2

5. Which number is the sum of 8 and 5?

A. 12   C. 14
B. 13   D. 15

2.OA.2

6. Which number completes the number sentence?

$$9 + 5 = ?$$

A. 17
B. 16
C. 15
D. 14

2.OA.2

TIP of the DAY

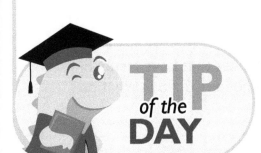

When adding two numbers, count from the larger number up to 10, then add on the rest of the smaller number. For some, it is easier to add from 10. For example, 9 + 3 = 10 + 2 = 12.

9 + 3 = 12

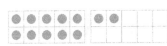

10 + 2 = 12

ASSESSMENT

1. Which number sentence does the model show?

   A. 7 + 7 = 14
   B. 7 + 8 = 15
   C. 8 + 8 = 16
   D. 8 + 9 = 17

   2.OA.2
   2.OA.4

2. Which number is the sum of 7 and 4?

   A. 10
   B. 11
   C. 12
   D. 13

   2.OA.2

3. Which 2 number pairs both have a sum of 10?

   A. 8 + 2 and 6 + 4
   B. 8 + 3 and 6 + 2
   C. 8 + 2 and 6 + 3
   D. 8 + 3 and 6 + 4

   2.OA.2

4. Which number sentence uses a double to find the sum?

   A. 4 + 6 = 10
   B. 5 + 6 = 11
   C. 5 + 7 = 12
   D. 6 + 6 = 12

   2.OA.2

5. Which pair of number sentences shows the order changed but the sum is the same?

   A. 9 + 3 = 12   4 + 8 = 12
   B. 9 + 3 = 12   3 + 9 = 12
   C. 8 + 4 = 12   2 + 10 = 12
   D. 12 + 0 = 12   1 + 11 = 12

   2.OA.2

6. Which pair of number sentences is shown in the model?

   ___ + ___ = ___   ___ + ___ = ___

   A. 9 + 9 = 9 + 9
   B. 9 + 9 = 10 + 8
   C. 9 + 9 = 10 + 9
   D. 9 + 9 = 10 + 10

   2.OA.2

DAY 6
Challenge question

What are 3 number sentences that have a sum of 14? Choose from the numbers 5 6 7 8 9. What do you notice?

2.OA.2

WEEK 4

This week we are subtracting single digit numbers. The numbers will go up to 18 - 9.

You can find detailed video explanations of each problem in the book by visiting:
ArgoPrep.com

1. Which number completes the number sentence:

$$10 - 6 = ?$$

A. 4
B. 6
C. 14
D. 16

2.OA.2

4. Which number sentence has a difference of 2?

A. $7 - 2 = ?$
B. $7 - 5 = ?$
C. $7 + 2 = ?$
D. $7 + 5 = ?$

2.OA.2

2. Which number is the difference of 9 and 4?

A. 4
B. 5
C. 13
D. 14

2.OA.2

5. Which number completes the number sentence?

$$12 - 6 = ?$$

A. 6
B. 8
C. 14
D. 18

2.OA.2

3. Which number sentence is related to the number sentence 6 + 7 = ?

A. $7 - 6 = 1$
B. $10 - 6 = 4$
C. $12 - 7 = 5$
D. $13 - 7 = 6$

2.OA.2

6. Which pair of number sentences is related?

A. $9 + 9 = 18$ and $9 - 9 = 0$
B. $9 + 9 = 18$ and $9 - 0 = 9$
C. $9 + 9 = 18$ and $18 - 9 = 9$
D. $9 + 9 = 18$ and $18 - 0 = 18$

2.OA.2

TIP of the DAY

Subtraction is related to addition.
For example, $5 + 2 = 7$, $7 - 5 = 2$ and $7 - 2 = 5$.
The same three numbers are in all of the number sentences. The answer to a subtraction problem is called the difference.

30

1. Which number completes the number sentence?

$$5 + ? = 12$$

A. 6
B. 7
C. 13
D. 17

2.OA.2

2. Which number sentence could be used to find the answer to $9 + ? = 17$

A. $9 - 8 = 1$
B. $16 - 9 = 7$
C. $17 - 9 = 8$
D. $18 - 9 = 9$

2.OA.2

3. Which number shows the difference of 15 and 6?

A. 1
B. 5
C. 8
D. 9

2.OA.2

4. Which number sentence is shown on the model?

3	?
7	

A. $7 - 3 = 4$
B. $7 + 3 = 10$
C. $10 - 7 = 3$
D. $7 - 1 = 6$

2.OA.2

5. Which number completes the number sentence?

$$8 + ? = 13$$

A. 4
B. 5
C. 6
D. 7

2.OA.2

6. Which number completes the number sentence?

$$14 - 7 = ?$$

A. 3
B. 4
C. 6
D. 7

2.OA.2

When finding the missing number in an addition problem, think of using a bar model to find the answer.

TIP of the DAY

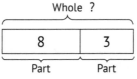

Whole ?

8	3
Part	Part

Add to find the whole $8 + 3 = 11$

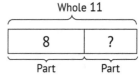

Whole 11

8	?
Part	Part

Substract to find the part $11 - 8 = 3$

31

1. The number line shows which number sentence?

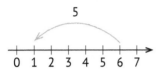

A. 6 − 1 = 5
B. 6 − 5 = 1
C. 6 + 5 = 11
D. 11 − 6 = 5.

2.OA.2

2. Which number is 4 more than 8?

A. 4   C. 12
B. 8   D. 16

2.OA.2

3. Which number sentence does the number line show?

A. 7 − 4 = 3   C. 11 + 4 = 15
B. 11 − 4 = 7   D. 11 + 7 = 18

2.OA.2

4. Which statement does the number line show?

A. 9 is 6 more than 3
B. 6 is 3 more than 3
C. 12 is 3 more than 9
D. 12 is 6 more than 6

2.OA.2

Use the number line to answer questions 5 and 6.

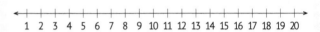

5. Which number is 7 more than 8?

A. 1   C. 14
B. 8   D. 15

2.OA.2

6. Which two numbers have a difference of 9?

A. 1 and 8   C. 5 and 14
B. 1 and 9   D. 9 and 17

2.OA.2

Subtracting numbers is also finding how far away two numbers are on a number line. We can also count up or back to find how much more or how much less numbers are from each other using the number line.

$14 - 6 = 8$

TIP
of the
DAY

When comparing the numbers 14 and 8 we see that they are 6 numbers apart on the number line. When we count back we see that 8 is 6 spaces less than 14 and when we count up we see that 14 is 6 spaces more than 8.

WEEK 4 : DAY 4

1. Which number sentence does the array show?

- **A.** 5 + 3 = 8
- **B.** 3 + 3 + 3 = 9
- **C.** 5 + 5 = 10
- **D.** 5 + 5 + 5 = 15

2.OA.4

2. Which number sentence does the array show?

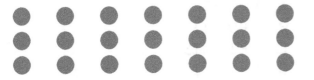

- **A.** 7 + 3 = 10
- **B.** 3 + 3 + 3 = 9
- **C.** 7 + 7 = 14
- **D.** 7 + 7 + 7 = 21

2.OA.4

3. Which number sentence does the array show?

- **A.** 2 + 6 = 8
- **B.** 4 + 4 = 8
- **C.** 2 + 2 + 2 + 2 + 2 + 2 = 12
- **D.** 4 + 4 + 4 + 4 = 16

2.OA.4

4. Which number sentence does this number line show?

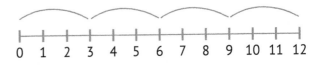

- **A.** 3 + 3 + 3 + 3 = 12
- **B.** 4 + 4 + 4 = 12
- **C.** 6 + 6 = 12
- **D.** 8 + 4 = 12

2.OA.2

5. Which number sentence could have an array to show the sum of 16?
- **A.** 2 + 2 + 4 + 4
- **B.** 4 + 4 + 4 + 4
- **C.** 4 + 4 + 8 + 8
- **D.** 8 + 8 + 8 + 8

2.OA.2

of the
TIP
DAY

We can use arrays and number lines to show addition that is repeated (done more than one time). For example the addition sentence 4 + 4 + 4 = ? can be shown using the array.

4 + 4 = 8 and 8 + 4 = 12 so 4 + 4 + 4 = 12.

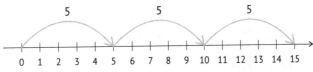

This number line shows 5 + 5 + 5 = 15

WEEK 4 : DAY 5

1. Which number sentence does the number line show?

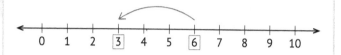

   A. $3 - 3 = 0$
   B. $3 + 6 = 9$
   C. $6 - 3 = 3$
   D. $0 + 6 = 6$

   2.OA.2

2. Which number sentence does the model show?

?	2

   8

   A. $8 - 2 = 6$
   B. $2 + 8 = 10$
   C. $12 - 4 = 8$
   D. $8 + 6 = 14$

   2.OA.2

3. Which number sentence does the array show?

   A. $6 + 4 = 10$
   B. $6 + 6 = 12$
   C. $4 + 4 + 4 + 4 = 16$
   D. $6 + 6 + 6 + 6 = 24$

   2.OA.2

4. Which number sentence could be used to find the answer to $13 - ? = 4$?

   A. $4 + 3 = 7$
   B. $4 + 9 = 13$
   C. $4 + 11 = 15$
   D. $4 + 13 = 17$

   2.OA.4

5. Which **two** number pairs **both** have a difference of 7?

   A. 7 and 1 and 14 and 7
   B. 7 and 0 and 14 and 7
   C. 7 and 7 and 16 and 9
   D. 7 and 1 and 16 and 9

   2.OA.2

DAY 6
Challenge question

Which 2 numbers have a sum of 15 and a difference of 1?

2.OA.2

34

WEEK 5

ARGOPREP.COM

VIDEO ▶
EXPLANATIONS

This week we are telling if numbers are even or odd. The numbers will go up to 2 digit numbers.

You can find detailed video explanations of each problem in the book by visiting:
ArgoPrep.com

WEEK 5 : DAY I

1. Which number is even?

    A. 3
    B. 4
    C. 5
    D. 7

2.OA.3

2. Which number is odd?

    A. 2
    B. 6
    C. 8
    D. 9

2.OA.3

3. Which numbers are both even?

    A. 1 and 2
    B. 3 and 6
    C. 8 and 10
    D. 9 and 10

2.OA.3

4. Which numbers are both odd?

    A. 1 and 3
    B. 2 and 5
    C. 3 and 6
    D. 4 and 7

2.OA.3

5. Which pair of numbers has one even and one odd number?

    A. 1 and 2
    B. 3 and 5
    C. 4 and 6
    D. 7 and 9

2.OA.1

6. Which statement is true?

    A. 1, 2, and 3 are all odd numbers.
    B. 2, 4, and 5 are all even numbers.
    C. 3, 5, and 7 are all odd numbers
    D. 7, 8, and 9 are all even numbers.

2.OA.3

TIP *of the* **DAY**

Even numbers can form pairs of two and odd numbers will have one left over.

2 is even   3 is odd   10 is even   7 is odd

1. In which pair of numbers are both numbers even?

    A. 3 and 10
    B. 4 and 15
    C. 6 and 18
    D. 7 and 14

2.OA.3

2. In which pair of numbers are both numbers odd?

    A. 4 and 13
    B. 5 and 17
    C. 6 and 11
    D. 7 and 18

2.OA.3

3. Starting with 10 and counting up, what are the next 2 odd numbers?

    A. 11 and 13
    B. 12 and 14
    C. 12 and 15
    D. 13 and 15

2.OA.3

4. Starting with 13 and counting up, what are the next 2 even numbers?

    A. 12 and 14
    B. 14 and 15
    C. 14 and 16
    D. 15 and 17

2.OA.3

5. Which set has all even numbers?

    A. 9, 10, 11, 12
    B. 9, 11, 12, 14
    C. 10, 13, 14, 15
    D. 12, 14, 16, 18

2.OA.3

6. Which set has all odd numbers?

    A. 11, 13, 15, 17
    B. 11, 12, 14, 16
    C. 12, 14, 17, 19
    D. 12, 15, 17, 19

2.OA.3

On a number line, 1 is an odd number, 2 is an even number, and the pattern continues: odd-even-odd-even. For greater numbers, the number in the ones place tells us what is even and odd. Numbers that end with 1, 3, 5, 7, and 9 are odd and numbers that end with 2, 4 6, 8, and 0 are even.

TIP *of the* **DAY**

odd even odd even odd even

1 2 3 4 5 6 7 8 9 10 11 12 13 14 15 16 17 18 19 20

WEEK 5 : DAY 3

1. Which sum is even?

- **A.** 2 + 3 = ?
- **B.** 3 + 4 = ?
- **C.** 4 + 4 = ?
- **D.** 4 + 5 = ?

2.OA.3

2. Which pair of equal even numbers has a sum of 16?

- **A.** 7 + 9
- **B.** 8 + 8
- **C.** 10 + 6
- **D.** 15 + 1

2.OA.3

3. Which pair of equal odd numbers has a sum of 14?

- **A.** 5 + 9
- **B.** 6 + 8
- **C.** 7 + 7
- **D.** 10 + 4

2.OA.3

4. Which number sentence makes the statement correct?

Odd + Odd = Even

- **A.** 7 + 7 = 14
- **B.** 7 + 8 = 15
- **C.** 8 + 8 = 16
- **D.** 8 + 9 = 17

2.OA.3

5. Which number sentence makes the statement correct?

Even + Even = Even

- **A.** 4 + 5 = 9
- **B.** 5 + 5 = 10
- **C.** 5 + 6 = 11
- **D.** 6 + 6 = 12

2.OA.3

TIP *of the* DAY

When adding two of the same numbers, no matter if they are both odd or both even, the sum is even.

2   +   2   =   4
even + even = even

3   +   3   =   6
odd + odd = even

38

1. Which number completes the number sentence?

$$? + 6 = 13$$

A. 6
B. 7
C. 9
D. 19

2.OA.2

2. Which number completes the number sentence?

$$? - 7 = 5$$

A. 2
B. 11
C. 12
D. 17

2.OA.2

3. Which number sentence could be used to find the answer?

$$? + 9 = 11$$

A. $11 - 9 = ?$ C. $11 + 9 = ?$
B. $11 + 2 = ?$ D. $20 - 9 = ?$

2.OA.2

4. Which number sentence could be used to find the answer?

$$? - 4 = 8$$

A. $8 - 4 = ?$
B. $8 + 4 = ?$
C. $12 + 4 = ?$
D. $12 + 8 = ?$

2.OA.2

5. Which number completes the number sentence?

$$? - 9 = 1$$

A. 8   C. 10
B. 9   D. 11

2.OA.2

When we don't know the first number in the number sentence, we can work backwards using the opposite of the sign.

$? + 5 = 14$	Working backwards,
$14 - 5 = ?$	$9 + 5 = 14$
$? - 8 = 7$	Working backwards,
$7 + 8 = 15$	$15 - 8 = 7$

TIP of the DAY

39

WEEK 5 : DAY 5

1. Which type of number sentence does the model show?

   A. Odd + Odd = Odd
   B. Odd + Odd = Even
   C. Odd + Even = Odd
   D. Odd + Even = Even

   2.OA.2

2. Which type of number sentence does the model show?

```
      ────────────►
  ┌─┬─┬─┬─┬─┬─┬─┬─┬─┬─┐
  0 1 2 3 4 5 6 7 8 9 10
```

   A. Odd + Odd = Odd
   B. Odd + Odd = Even
   C. Odd + Even = Odd
   D. Even + Even = Even

   2.OA.2

3. Which type of number sentence is shown?

$$8 + 8 = 16$$

   A. Odd + Odd = Odd
   B. Odd + Odd = Even
   C. Odd + Even = Odd
   D. Even + Even = Even

   2.OA.2

4. Which set of numbers has two even and one odd number in the set?

   A. 8, 10, 12
   B. 9, 11, 13
   C. 10, 11, 14
   D. 11, 12, 15

   2.OA.2

5. Which number completes the number sentence?

$$? + 6 = 15$$

   A. 1
   B. 9
   C. 11
   D. 21

   2.OA.2

6. Which number sentence could be used to find the answer?

$$? - 9 = 8$$

   A. 9 − 8 = ?
   B. 1 + 9 = ?
   C. 8 + 1 = ?
   D. 8 + 9 = ?

   2.OA.2

DAY 6
Challenge question

What happens when you add an odd number and an even number? Odd + Even = ?
Give some examples.
Explain why.

2.OA.2

WEEK 6

This week we are using addition and subtraction to solve problems. The numbers will go up to 100.

You can find detailed video explanations of each problem in the book by visiting:
ArgoPrep.com

1. There were 40 cars parked in the front of the school. In the back there were 53 cars. Which shows the total amount of cars in the front and the back?

   A. 7   **C.** 53
   B. 13   **D.** 93

   2.OA.1

2. At lunch 25 girls were sitting at the big tables. There were 10 boys sitting at the big tables. How many more girls than boys were sitting at the big tables?

   A. 5
   B. 15
   C. 25
   D. 35

   2.OA.1

3. The teacher has 17 red notebooks and 30 blue notebooks. How many total notebooks does the teacher have?

   A. 13   **C.** 20
   B. 17   **D.** 47

   2.OA.1

4. In the class there were 40 crayons in boxes. There were 25 crayons not in boxes. How many total crayons were in the class?

   A. 15
   B. 25
   C. 65
   D. 85

   2.OA.1

5. In the big box there are 48 pencils. In the small box there are 20 pencils. How many more pencils are in the big box?

   A. 20   **C.** 50
   B. 28   **D.** 68

   2.OA.1

6. A total of 62 children were outside playing. Then 30 children went into the school. How many children were still outside playing?

   A. 30   **C.** 65
   B. 32   **D.** 92

   2.OA.1

When solving word problems by adding and subtracting, making models such as bar models and number bonds are helpful.

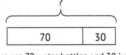

There are 70 water bottles and 30 juice bottles. How many bottles in all?

70 + 30 = 100 bottles

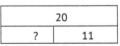

There were 20 children on the bus. Then 11 children got off the bus. How many children are now on the bus?

20 – 11 = 9 children

There are 21 new pencils and 27 old pencils in the box. How many total pencils are in the box?

21 + 27 = 48 pencils

of the
TIP
DAY

42

WEEK 6 : DAY 2

1. Which is the sum of 33 + 44?

A. 37
B. 47
C. 77
D. 87

2.NBT.5
2.NBT.6

2. Which number is the total of 28 + 41?

A. 29
B. 49
C. 59
D. 69

2.NBT.5
2.NBT.6

3. Which number is the difference of 64 and 23?

A. 40
B. 41
C. 61
D. 87

2.NBT.5
2.NBT.6

4. Which number is 20 less than 78?

A. 50
B. 58
C. 80
D. 98

2.NBT.5
2.NBT.6

5. Which number is 20 more than 37?

A. 17
B. 35
C. 39
D. 57

2.NBT.5
2.NBT.6

6. Which number completes the number sentence?

20 + 31 + 42 = ?

A. 51
B. 73
C. 75
D. 93

2.NBT.5
2.NBT.6

TIP *of the* **DAY**

When adding 2 digit numbers, put the numbers neatly into columns. Add or subtract the ones and then the tens.

```
  25        48
+ 50      - 17
-----      -----
  75        31
```

43

1. Which number completes the number sentence?

$$39 + 23 = ?$$

A. 16
B. 50
C. 52
D. 62

2.NBT.5

2. Which number is the sum of 48 and 32?

A. 16
B. 70
C. 76
D. 80

2.NBT.5

3. Which number is 15 more than 78?

A. 63
B. 73
C. 83
D. 93

2.NBT.5

4. Which number completes the number sentence?

$$39 + 12 = ?$$

A. 27
B. 41
C. 51
D. 61

2.NBT.5

5. Which number is the sum of 67 and 6?

A. 61
B. 63
C. 73
D. 91

2.NBT.5

6. Which number is 23 more than 59?

A. 36
B. 72
C. 82
D. 91

2.NBT.5

When adding, sometimes the sum of the ones place is a 2 digit number (tens and ones), so we need to place the tens digit into the tens place.

TIP *of the* **DAY**

```
    +1
    28      20 + 8
  + 17      10 + 7
  ────      ──────
    45      30 + 15  (place the 1 in the 15 above the tens place)
```

1. Which number completes the number sentence?

$$52 - 25 = ?$$

A. 23
B. 27
C. 33
D. 37

2.NBT.5

4. Which number completes the number sentence?

$$40 - 28 = ?$$

A. 12
B. 22
C. 28
D. 68

2.NBT.5

2. Which number is the difference of 71 and 42?

A. 21
B. 29
C. 31
D. 39

2.NBT.5

5. Which number is the difference of 35 and 6?

A. 29
B. 31
C. 39
D. 41

2.NBT.5

3. Which number is 36 less than 64?

A. 22
B. 28
C. 32
D. 38

2.NBT.5

6. Which number is 23 less than 42?

A. 11
B. 19
C. 21
D. 29

2.NBT.5

When subtracting, sometimes the first number needs to be renamed so that you can subtract. Be sure to check and rename the number.

of the

TIP
DAY

```
   4  13
   5̶3̶       5 tens 3 ones      4 tens 13 ones
 − 16        1 ten  6 ones      1 ten   6 ones
 ─────                          ──────────────
   37                           3 tens   7 ones
```

45

1. There were 23 soccer players and 26 football players. How many total players were there?

   A. 43
   B. 49
   C. 53
   D. 59

   2.OA.1

2. A total of 36 cans of soda were on the table. The children drank 25 cans. How many cans of soda were now left on the table?

   A. 1
   B. 11
   C. 51
   D. 61

   2.OA.1

3. Which number completes the number sentence?

   $$41 + 42 + 12 = ?$$

   A. 54
   B. 83
   C. 85
   D. 95

   2.NBT.6

4. Which number is the difference of 81 and 13?

   A. 68
   B. 72
   C. 78
   D. 94

   2.NBT.5

5. Which number is 16 less than 50?

   A. 34
   B. 44
   C. 46
   D. 66

   2.NBT.5

6. Which number is 18 more than 58?

   A. 30
   B. 40
   C. 66
   D. 76

   2.NBT.5

DAY 6
Challenge question

Find two numbers with a sum of 75.
Find the difference of the same two numbers.

WEEK 7

This week we are adding and subtracting larger numbers from tables and models.
The numbers will go up to 100.

You can find detailed video explanations of each problem in the book by visiting:
ArgoPrep.com

1. Which number completes the addition problem?

   A. 59
   B. 76
   C. 90
   D. 100

   $$\begin{array}{r} 24 \\ 35 \\ +\ 41 \\ \hline \end{array}$$

   2.NBT.6

2. Which number is the sum of 12, 35 and 5?

   A. 42   C. 61
   B. 52   D. 97

   2.NBT.6

3. Which number completes the number sentence? 14 + 28 + 42 = ?

   A. 70   C. 84
   B. 74   D. 111

   2.NBT.6

The number of children that are in the Art Club is shown in the table.
Use the table to complete questions 4, 5 and 6

Number of Children in Art Club

Grade	Number of Boys	Number of Girls
1	16	17
2	15	18
3	21	21

4. Which shows the total number of boys in the Art Club?

   A. 42
   B. 51
   C. 52
   D. 61

   2.NBT.1
   2.NBT.6

5. Which shows the total number of girls in the Art Club?

   A. 41
   B. 46
   C. 55
   D. 56

   2.NBT.1
   2.NBT.6

6. Which shows the total number of children in Grades 2 and 3 in the Art Club?

   A. 54
   B. 57
   C. 65
   D. 75

   2.NBT.1
   2.NBT.6

TIP of the DAY

When adding more than 2 numbers, add two numbers, then keep adding on to the sum.
15 add 5 + 6 = 11, then 11 + 7 = 18, don't forget to regroup the 1

$$\begin{array}{r} 16 \\ +\ 17 \\ \hline 48 \end{array}$$

WEEK 7 : DAY 2

At a school, there are 4 teams that play a game each day. The table shows the teams and the number of points scored in the first 4 games. Use the table to answer questions 1-6

Points Scored by Each Team in Each Game

Game	Red Team	Blue Team	Green Team	White Team
1	17	16	13	14
2	10	13	14	17
3	14	20	21	7
4	21	17	16	20

1. Which shows the total number of points scored by the Red team?

   A. 45
   B. 52
   C. 62
   D. 66

   2.OA.1
   2.OA.2
   2.NBT.6

2. Which shows the total number of points scored by the Blue team?

   A. 49
   B. 56
   C. 62
   D. 66

   2.OA.1
   2.OA.2
   2.NBT.6

3. Which shows the total number of points scored by the Green team?

   A. 48   C. 58
   B. 54   D. 64

   2.OA.1
   2.OA.2
   2.NBT.6

4. Which shows the total number of points scored by the White team?

   A. 48   C. 58
   B. 54   D. 64

   2.OA.1
   2.OA.2
   2.NBT.6

5. Which team scored the greatest total of points for the 4 games?

   A. Red   C. Green
   B. Blue   D. White

   2.OA.1
   2.OA.2
   2.NBT.6

6. Which team scored the least total of points for the 4 games?

   A. Red
   B. Blue
   C. Green
   D. White

   2.OA.1
   2.OA.2
   2.NBT.6

When using numbers in a table to add, make sure you find the right numbers to add.

Flowers in Garden

Flower Color	Red	Yellow	Pink	White
Number of Flowers	13	14	15	16

How many yellow and pink flowers are in the garden?
Only look for the numbers for yellow and pink.

$$\begin{array}{r} 14 \\ + 15 \\ \hline 29 \end{array}$$

pink and yellow flowers

TIP
of the
DAY

49

The teacher has new boxes of pens, pencils, crayons and markers. The table shows the number of pens, pencils, crayons and markers that are in each new box.

Use the table to answer questions 1-5

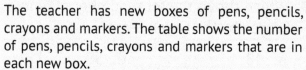

	Pens	Pencils	Crayons	Markers
Number in Each Box	14	26	32	18

3. Which shows the total number of pens and pencils for 1 box of pens and 2 boxes of pencils?

   A. 54
   B. 66
   C. 70
   D. 80

   2.OA.1
   2.NBT.6

1. Which shows the total number of pens and pencils for 2 boxes of each?

   A. 40
   B. 50
   C. 70
   D. 80

   2.OA.1
   2.NBT.6

4. Which shows the total number of crayons and markers for 1 box of crayons and 2 boxes of markers?

   A. 68
   B. 82
   C. 90
   D. 100

   2.OA.1
   2.NBT.6

2. Which shows the total number of crayons and markers for 2 boxes of each?

   A. 50
   B. 80
   C. 90
   D. 100

   2.OA.1
   2.NBT.6

5. Which shows the total number for 1 box of pens, pencils, crayons and markers?

   A. 72
   B. 76
   C. 80
   D. 90

   2.OA.1
   2.NBT.6

TIP of the DAY

When adding more than 2 numbers, look for numbers that add up to 10 and add them together first.
You can add 4 + 6 = 10, then add 10 + 2 = 12.

```
  14
  12
+ 16
  42
```

1. Last year there were 418 children in the school. This year there are 100 more. Which shows the number of children in the school this year?

   A. 318
   B. 408
   C. 428
   D. 518

   2.OA.1
   2.NBT.8

2. There were 231 people at the game. Then 10 people left. How many people are now at the game?

   A. 131
   B. 221
   C. 241
   D. 331

   2.OA.1
   2.NBT.8

3. Which number is 10 more than 567?

   A. 467
   B. 557
   C. 577
   D. 667

   2.OA.1
   2.NBT.8

4. Which number completes the number sentence?

   $$? + 100 = 725$$

   A. 625
   B. 715
   C. 735
   D. 825

   2.OA.1
   2.NBT.8

5. Which number completes the number sentence?

   $$? - 10 = 341$$

   A. 241
   B. 331
   C. 351
   D. 441

   2.OA.1
   2.NBT.8

6. Which number completes the number sentence?

   $$? + 10 = 819$$

   A. 719
   B. 809
   C. 829
   D. 919

   2.OA.1
   2.NBT.8

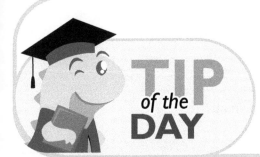

TIP of the DAY

When adding or subtracting 10 more, 10 less, 100 more or 100 less, make sure that you place the numbers in the right place.

	Incorrect	Correct
Add: 249 + 10	249	249
	+10	+ 10
	349	259

1. There are 16 clips in a small box.
   There are 24 clips in a big box.
   How many total clips are in 2 small boxes and 1 large box?

   A. 46   C. 70
   B. 56   D. 80

2. Which number completes the number sentence?

   $$42 + 33 + 8 = ?$$

   A. 83
   B. 113
   C. 122
   D. 155

3. Ava counted the number of birds that she saw each day for 4 days. The table shows the day and the number of birds.

Day	1	2	3	4
Number of Birds	15	4	7	23

   Which shows the total number of birds that Ava saw for the 4 days?

   A. 39   C. 75
   B. 49   D. 85

4. Which number is 100 more than 540?

   A. 440
   B. 530
   C. 550
   D. 640

5. Which number is 10 less than 723?

   A. 623
   B. 713
   C. 733
   D. 823

6. Which number completes the number sentence?

   $$? - 10 = 172$$

   A. 72
   B. 162
   C. 182
   D. 272

DAY 6
Challenge question

Last week the class brought in 53 cans.
Then they brought in 100 more.
Then they brought in 10 more.
Then they brought in 100 more.
Now how many cans are there in all?

WEEK 8

VIDEO EXPLANATIONS

ARGOPREP.COM

This week we are using what we know about place value to add and subtract large numbers. The numbers will go up to 1,000.

You can find detailed video explanations of each problem in the book by visiting: ArgoPrep.com

WEEK 8 : DAY 1

1. Which number completes the number sentence?

$$250 + 43 = ?$$

A. 68
B. 257
C. 293
D. 680

2.NBT.7

2. Which number completes the number sentence?

$$269 - 21 = ?$$

A. 59
B. 149
C. 248
D. 280

2.NBT.7

3. Which number is the sum of 303 + 415?

A. 112
B. 448
C. 718
D. 745

2.NBT.7

4. Which number is the difference of 678 and 210?

A. 468
B. 657
C. 699
D. 888

2.NBT.7

5. Which number completes the number sentence?

$$? + 140 = 354$$

A. 214
B. 340
C. 368
D. 494

2.NBT.7

6. Which number completes the number sentence?

$$? - 103 = 203$$

A. 100
B. 216
C. 303
D. 306

2.NBT.7

TIP of the DAY

When adding 3 digit numbers, make sure you line up the numbers in the right place.

$123 + 45 = ?$

Incorrect	Correct
123	123
+ 45	+ 45
573	168

WEEK 8 : DAY 2

1. Which number is the sum of 363 and 252?

     3 hundreds   6 tens   3 ones
+ 2 hundreds   5 tens   2 ones

- **A.** 111
- **B.** 211
- **C.** 515
- **D.** 615

2.NBT.7

2. The model can be used to find which sum?

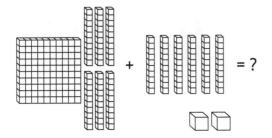

- **A.** 78
- **B.** 122
- **C.** 222
- **D.** 780

2.NBT.7

3. Which number sentence does the model show?

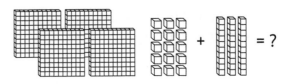

- **A.** 415 + 3 = 418
- **B.** 415 + 30 = 445
- **C.** 450 + 3 = 453
- **D.** 450 + 30 = 480

2.NBT.7

4. The chart can be used to find which sum?

     5 hundreds   7 tens   4 ones
+ 1 hundreds   4 tens   2 ones

- **A.** 332   **C.** 616
- **B.** 432   **D.** 716

2.NBT.7

5. The model can be used to find which sum?

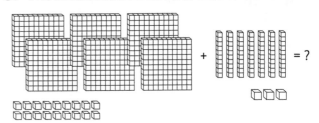

- **A.** 142   **C.** 691
- **B.** 151   **D.** 763

2.NBT.7

TIP of the DAY

Use place value charts or models to add when you need to regroup to the next place.

  644 6 hundreds   4 tens 4 ones
+ 172 1 hundred   7 tens 2 ones
  816 7 hundreds 11 tens 6 ones or
        8 hundreds   1 ten   6 ones

1. Which number completes the number sentence 540 – 250?

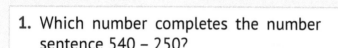

   5 hundreds 4 tens or 4 hundreds 14 tens
   – 2 hundreds 5 tens – 2 hundreds   5 tens

   A. 210
   B. 290
   C. 310
   D. 390

   2.NBT.7

2. The model can be used for which number sentence?

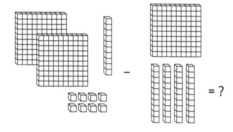

   A. 218 – 14 = 204
   B. 218 – 140 = 78
   C. 281 – 14 = 267
   D. 281 – 140 = 141

   2.NBT.7

3. Which number completes the number sentence 906 – 415?

   906 9 hundreds 0 tens 6 ones or 8 hundreds 10 tens 6 ones
   – 415 4 hundreds 1 ten   5 ones –   4 hundreds   1 ten   5
   ones

   A. 491
   B. 501
   C. 511
   D. 591

   2.NBT.7

4. The model can be used to find which difference?

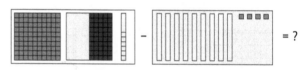

   A. 62   **C.** 162
   B. 140   **D.** 250

   2.NBT.7

5. Which number completes the number sentence?

   2 hundreds 4 tens 3 ones = 2 hundreds _?_ tens __?_ ones
   – 1 hundred 2 tens   5 ones – 1 hundred   2 tens   5 ones

   A. 3 tens and 3 ones
   B. 3 tens and 13 ones
   C. 5 tens and 3 ones
   D. 4 tens and 13 ones

   2.NBT.7

TIP
of the
DAY

Use charts or models when you need to regroup for subtraction.
   613 6 hundreds 1 ten   3 ones or 5 hundreds 11 tens 3 ones
   – 382 3 hundreds 8 tens 2 ones   3 hundreds   8 tens 2 ones
   231   2 hundreds   3 tens 1 one

WEEK 8 : DAY 4

Use the model for question 1 and 2.

First Number   Second Number

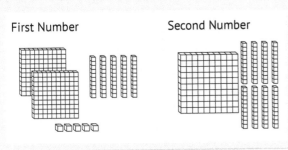

1. Which number is the sum of the first and second number?

   A. 273   **C.** 363

   B. 335   **D.** 435   2.NBT.7

2. Which number is the difference of the first and second number?

   A. 75   **C.** 175

   B. 147   **D.** 237

                          2.NBT.7

Use the model for questions 3 and 4.

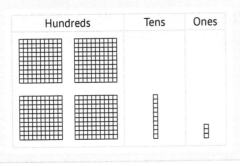

Hundreds	Tens	Ones

3. Which shows the sum of the number in the model and 251?

   A. 664   **C.** 682

   B. 674   **D.** 764   2.NBT.7

4. Which shows the difference of the number in the model and 251?

   A. 152   **C.** 252

   B. 162   **D.** 262   2.NBT.7

Use the model for questions 5 and 6.

First Number

Second Number

5. Which shows the sum of the first number and the second number?

   A. 314   **C.** 414

   B. 324   **D.** 424   2.NBT.7

6. Which shows the difference of the first number and the second number?

   A. 28   **C.** 128

   B. 32   **D.** 132   2.NBT.7

TIP of the DAY

Be sure to check the sign to determine if you will be adding (finding the sum), or subtracting (finding the difference).

WEEK 8 : DAY 5

ASSESSMENT

1. Which number completes the number sentence?

$$710 + 208 = ?$$

A. 908   C. 981
B. 918   D. 990

2.NBT.7

2. Which number completes the number sentence?

$$638 - 23 = ?$$

A. 408   C. 606
B. 435   D. 615

2.NBT.7

3. Which number is the sum of 429 + 414?

   4 hundreds __ 2 tens __ 9 ones
 + 4 hundreds   1 ten   4 ones
 _____

A. 833   C. 933
B. 843   D. 943

2.NBT.7

4. Which number is the difference of 537 and 218?

 5 hundreds 3 tens 7 ones or 5 hundreds 2 tens 17 ones
 - 2 hundreds 1 ten   8 ones - 2 hundreds 1 ten 8 ones
 _____

A. 219   C. 319
B. 229   D. 329

2.NBT.7

Use the model for questions 5 and 6.

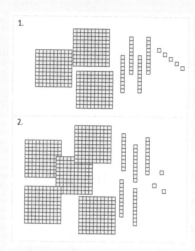

5. Which shows the sum of the first number and the second number?

A. 808
B. 898
C. 908
D. 998

2.NBT.7

6. Which shows the difference of the first number and the second number?

A. 108
B. 112
C. 208
D. 212

2.NBT.7

DAY 6
Challenge question

Find the difference between 678 and 123.
What do you notice?

WEEK 9

ARGOPREP.COM

VIDEO ▶
EXPLANATIONS

This week we are finding different ways to add and subtract numbers. Numbers will use base ten models and place value charts.

You can find detailed video explanations of each problem in the book by visiting:
ArgoPrep.com

WEEK 9 : DAY 1

1. Which number completes the number sentence?

$$4 + 7 = 10 + ?$$

A. 1
B. 2
C. 10
D. 11

1.OA.7
2.OA.2

2. Which number completes the number sentence?

$$8 + 8 = 10 \_\_ \_\_ ?$$

A. - 4
B. + 4
C. - 6
D. + 6

1.OA.7
2.OA.2

3. Which number completes the number sentence?

$$6 + 8 = 10 + ?$$

A. 2
B. 4
C. 10
D. 16

1.OA.7
2.OA.2

4. Which number completes the number sentence?

$$7 + 8 = 9 \_\_ \_\_ ?$$

A. add 6
B. subtract 6
C. add 15
D. subtract 15

1.OA.7
2.OA.2

5. Which number completes the number sentence?

$$9 + 8 = 14 + ?$$

A. 3
B. 5
C. 6
D. 17

1.OA.7
2.OA.2

6. Which number completes the number sentence?

$$6 + 9 = 8 + ?$$

A. 1
B. 2
C. 5
D. 7

1.OA.7
2.OA.2

TIP of the DAY

When finding the answer for longer number sentences, find the answer on one side of the equal sign first. Which number completes the number sentence?

$$3 + 9 = 10 + ?$$

Solve $3 + 9 = 12$ $12 = 10 + ?$ Answer: 2

WEEK 9 : DAY 2

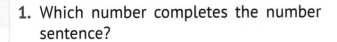

1. Which number completes the number sentence?

$$8 + 8 = 19 - ?$$

A. 3
B. 8
C. 11
D. 16

1.OA.7
2.OA.2

4. Which number completes the number sentence?

$$9 + 7 = 25 \underline{\ } \underline{\ \ } ?$$

A. add 9
B. add 16
C. subtract 9
D. subtract 16

1.OA.7
2.OA.1

2. Which number and sign completes the number sentence?

$$7 + 5 = 18 \underline{\ } \underline{\ \ } ?$$

A. +6
B. -6
C. +15
D. -15

1.OA.7
2.OA.2

5. Which number completes the number sentence?

$$9 + 9 = ? - 2$$

A. 7
B. 11
C. 18
D. 20

1.OA.7
2.OA.1

3. Which number completes the number sentence?

$$4 + 9 = 17 - ?$$

A. 3
B. 4
C. 8
D. 13

1.OA.7
2.OA.2

6. Which number completes the number sentence?

$$9 + 8 = ? - 5$$

A. 13
B. 14
C. 17
D. 22

1.OA.7
2.OA.1

TIP of the DAY

Check the signs in the number sentence when finding the answer.
$$5 + 5 = 14 - ?$$

First, add the left side $\quad 5 + 5 = 10 \quad\quad 10 = 14 - ?$
Now we will subtract to find what equals 10. $\quad 14 - 4 = 10.$ $\quad ? = 4$

1. Which number completes the number sentence?

$$20 + 15 = ? + 10$$

A. 10
B. 15
C. 25
D. 35

2.OA.1

4. Which number completes the number sentence?

$$52 + 20 = 88 - ?$$

A. 16
B. 36
C. 68
D. 72

2.OA.1

2. Which number and sign completes the number sentence?

$$40 + 8 = 60 \_\_ \_\_ ?$$

A. + 48
B. - 48
C. + 12
D. - 12

2.OA.1

5. Which sign and number completes the number sentence?

$$75 - 30 = 25 \_\_ \_\_ ?$$

A. + 20
B. - 5
C. - 20
D. + 50

2.OA.1

3. Which number completes the number sentence?

$$33 + 10 = 20 + ?$$

A. 3
B. 10
C. 23
D. 43

2.OA.1

6. Which number completes the number sentence?

$$35 + 35 = 95 - ?$$

A. 25
B. 35
C. 60
D. 70

2.OA.1

TIP of the DAY

When you find the answer, do the problem again with your answer to see if it is correct.

$4 + 10 = 30 - ?$
$4 + 10 = 14$ $30 - ? = 14$ $30 - 14 = 16$
$4 + 10 = 30 - 16$ $14 = 14$

1. Which number completes the number sentence?

$$44 - 20 = 10 + ?$$

A. 10
B. 14
C. 24
D. 34

2.OA.1

2. Which could tell us how to complete the number sentence?

$$80 - 22 = 20 \underline{} \underline{} ?$$

A. add 38
B. add 58
C. subtract 60
D. subtract 102

2.OA.1

3. Which number completes the number sentence?

$$45 + 25 = \underline{} \underline{} 30 ?$$

A. 70 +
B. 70 -
C. 100 +
D. 100 -

2.OA.1

4. Which number completes the number sentence?

$$84 - 40 = 20 + ?$$

A. 20
B. 24
C. 44
D. 60

2.OA.1

5. Which number completes the number sentence?

$$15 + 30 = 35 + ?$$

A. 5
B. 10
C. 15
D. 20

2.OA.1

6. Which number and sign complete the number sentence?

$$20 + 30 + 25 = \underline{} \underline{} 25$$

A. 50 -
B. 50 +
C. 75 -
D. 75 +

2.OA.1

TIP of the DAY

Be sure to check your work.

WEEK 9 : DAY 5

1. Which number completes the number sentence?

$$6 + 7 = 10 + ?$$

A. 3
B. 4
C. 13
D. 17

1.OA.7
2.OA.1

2. Which number completes the number sentence?

$$7 + 7 = 18 \ \_\_ \ \_\_ \ ?$$

A. - 4
B. + 4
C. - 14
D. + 14

1.OA.7
2.OA.1

3. Which number completes the number sentence?

$$30 + 16 = 26 + ?$$

A. 4
B. 10
C. 20
D. 46

1.OA.7
2.OA.1

4. Which could tell us how to complete the number sentence?

$$84 - 45 = 32 \ \_\_ \ \_\_ \ ?$$

A. add 7
B. add 40
C. subtract 8
D. subtract 40

1.OA.7
2.OA.1

5. Which number completes the number sentence?

$$79 - 30 = 39 + ?$$

A. 9
B. 10
C. 30
D. 49

1.OA.7
2.OA.1

6. Which number and sign complete the number sentence?

$$10 + 20 + 30 = \ \_\_ \ \_\_ \ 30$$

A. 30 +
B. 30 -
C. 60 +
D. 60 -

1.OA.7
2.OA.1

DAY 6
Challenge question

A. Find the sum of the numbers shown.
$$50 + 25 + 5 = ?$$

B. Find the same sum using two numbers.
$$\_\_\_\_ + \_\_\_\_ = ?$$

This week we are reviewing what we know from weeks 1-9. You can review weeks 1-9 to make sure you remember all of the skills.

You can find detailed video explanations of each problem in the book by visiting:
ArgoPrep.com

WEEK 10 : DAY 1

1. Which set of numbers completes the sentence?

The number 395 has ?

A. 3 hundreds 5 tens and 9 ones
B. 3 hundreds 9 tens and 3 ones
C. 3 hundreds 9 tens and 5 ones
D. 3 hundreds 5 tens and 5 ones

2.OA
2.NBT

2. Which set of numbers completes the sentence?

The number 702 has ?

A. 7 tens and 2 ones
B. 2 tens and 7 hundreds
C. 7 hundreds and 2 tens
D. 2 ones and 7 hundreds

2.OA
2.NBT

3. Which number completes the sentence?

The number ? has 5 tens and 8 hundreds

A. 58
B. 85
C. 805
D. 850

2.OA
2.NBT

4. Which number completes the number sentence?

Six hundred four > ?

A. 6 hundreds 3 tens 0 ones
B. 6 hundreds 1 ten 3 ones
C. 6 hundreds 0 tens 3 ones
D. 6 hundreds 0 tens 6 ones

2.OA
2.NBT

5. Which number completes the number sentence?

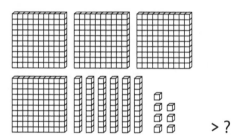 > ?

A. Four hundred sixty one
B. Four hundred sixty seven
C. Four hundred seventy six
D. Four hundred seventy seven

2.OA
2.NBT

6. Which sign completes the number sentence?

8 hundreds 1 ten nine ones ? 8 hundred twenty eight

A. >   B. <   C. =

2.OA
2.NBT

TIP
of the
DAY

When doing different kinds of problems, take time to remember similar problems that you did before.

WEEK 10 : DAY 2

1. Jake had 7 crayons in a box. He put 8 more crayons in the box. Which shows the number of crayons that Jake has now?

   A. 1
   B. 7
   C. 14
   D. 15

   2.OA.2

2. Sam had 16 stickers. She gave 7 stickers to her friend. Which shows the number of stickers that Sam has now?

   A. 8
   B. 9
   C. 10
   D. 23

   2.OA.2

3. Which shows the sum of 9 and 8?

   A. 1
   B. 8
   C. 17
   D. 18

   2.OA.2

4. Which shows the difference of 9 and 8?

   A. 1
   B. 8
   C. 17
   D. 18

   2.OA.2

5. Which number completes the number sentence?

   $$8 + 6 = ?$$

   A. 2
   B. 12
   C. 13
   D. 14

   2.OA.2

6. Which number completes the number sentence?

   $$15 - 6 = ?$$

   A. 9
   B. 11
   C. 19
   D. 21

   2.OA.2

TIP of the DAY

Practicing math daily will help you significantly increase your understanding of different math topics and help you feel confident for any quizzes or tests.

WEEK 10 : DAY 3

1. Which sentences are all TRUE about the array shown?

   A. The array shows 6 + 5 and the answer is odd.
   B. The array shows 6 + 6 and the answer is even.
   C. The array shows 5 + 5 + 5 + 5 + 5 and the answer is odd.
   D. The array shows 6 + 6 + 6 + 6 + 6 and the answer is even.

2.OA.4

2. Which number sentence is shown using the model?

   A. 7 + ? = 21
   B. 7 + 21 = ?
   C. 7 + 7 = ?
   D. 21 + 14 = ?

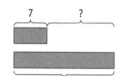

2.OA.1

Use the model for #3 - #4.

3. Which shows the sum of the number in the model and 150?

   A. 281
   B. 291
   C. 326
   D. 426

2.OA.7

4. Which shows the difference of the number in the model and 150?

   A. 26
   B. 61
   C. 126
   D. 261

2.OA.7

5. Which number is 10 less than 844?

   A. 744
   B. 834
   C. 854
   D. 944

2.OA.8

6. Which number is 100 more than 632?

   A. 532
   B. 622
   C. 642
   D. 732

2.OA.8

TIP of the DAY

Yesterday, we talked about how important daily math practice is. A good night's sleep is also just as important to keep your math skills sharp.

68

1. Kesha has 13 red bows, 14 blue bows and 15 green bows. Which shows the total number of bows that Kesha has?

   A. 27
   B. 29
   C. 32
   D. 42

   2.OA.6

2. There are 63 water bottles. The coach gave 27 water bottles to the children. Which shows the number of water bottles that are left?

   A. 36
   B. 44
   C. 46
   D. 90

   2.OA.5

3. Ali has 4 boxes of toy cars. Each box has 8 toy cars. Which number sentence could be used to find the total number of toy cars in the 4 boxes?

   A. 4 + 4 + 4 = ?
   B. 4 + 4 + 4 + 4 = ?
   C. 8 + 8 + 8 + 8 = ?
   D. 4 + 8 + 4 + 8 = ?

   2.OA.4

4. There are 12 cookies in the small box. There are 24 cookies is the big box. How many total cookies are in 2 small boxes and 2 big boxes?

   A. 24   C. 48
   B. 36   D. 72

   2.OA.6

5. There are 3 bags of grapes. Two bags have 31 grapes. The other bag has 35 grapes. Which shows the total number of grapes in the 3 bags?

   A. 72   C. 97
   B. 93   D. 105

   2.OA.6

6. The football team played 4 games. The table shows the number of points scored in each game.

Game	1	2	3	4
Points Scored	10	14	7	17

   Which shows the total number of points scored in the 4 games?

   A. 31
   B. 38
   C. 48
   D. 111

   2.OA.6

TIP of the DAY

If you are stuck on one question, move on and complete the other questions. Then, come back to the question and try to solve it. If you are still stuck, don't forget we have detailed video explanations on our website.

Use the models below for questions 1-4.

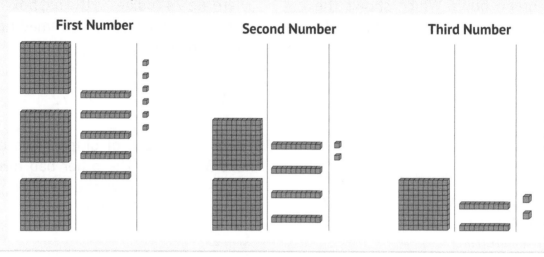

First Number   Second Number   Third Number

1. Which number shows the sum of the First and Second Numbers?

   A. 364   **C.** 598
   B. 478   **D.** 720

2. Which shows the difference of the Second and Third Numbers?

   A. 110
   B. 114
   C. 120
   D. 234

3. Which shows the number that is 100 more than the Second Number?

   A. 142   **C.** 256
   B. 222   **D.** 342

4. Which shows the sum of all three numbers?

   A. 710   **C.** 810
   B. 720   **D.** 820

5. Which number completes the number sentence?

$$68 - 20 = 18 + ?$$

   A. 30   **C.** 48
   B. 38   **D.** 50

2.OA.5

6. Which number completes the number sentence?

$$26 + 31 = 77 - ?$$

   A. 20   **C.** 51
   B. 46   **D.** 57

2.OA.5

Mid Assessment

VIDEO
EXPLANATIONS

ARGOPREP.COM

You can find detailed video explanations of each problem in the book by visiting:
ArgoPrep.com

MID ASSESSMENT

1. There were 7 apples in a bag. Then 8 more apples were put in the bag. Which shows the total number of apples?

   A. 14
   B. 15
   C. 16
   D. 17

   2.OA.2

2. Don had 13 baseball cards. He gave 5 to some friends. Which shows the number of baseball cards that Don has left?

   A. 8
   B. 9
   C. 12
   D. 18

   2.OA.2

3. Which number completes the number sentence?

   $$7 + 4 = 10 + ?$$

   A. 1
   B. 3
   C. 6
   D. 11

   2.OA.2

4. Which number completes the number sentence?

   $$6 + 6 = ?$$

   A. 6 + 2
   B. 6 + 4
   C. 10 + 2
   D. 10 + 4

   2.OA.2

5. Which set of numbers are all even?

   A. 2, 3, 4, 5
   B. 2, 4, 5, 7
   C. 2, 6, 9, 12
   D. 2, 6, 10, 12

   2.OA.3

6. Which number sentence has a sum that is odd?

   A. 4 + 2 = ?
   B. 4 + 4 = ?
   C. 4 + 5 = ?
   D. 4 + 6 = ?

   2.OA.3

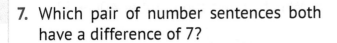

7. Which pair of number sentences both have a difference of 7?

A. 7 – 7 = ? and 9 – 2 = ?
B. 8 – 1 = ? and 9 – 2 = ?
C. 8 – 7 = ? and 10 – 3 = ?
D. 8 – 1 = ? and 10 – 7 = ?

2.OA.2

8. Which number sentence could be used to find the answer to 9 + ? = 15?

A. 9 + 4 = ?
B. 15 – 4 = ?
C. 15 – 9 = ?
D. 9 + 15 = ?

2.OA.2

9. In the morning there were 84 toy bears in a store. Then 38 toy bears were sold.

Which shows the number of toy bears now in the store?

A. 44
B. 46
C. 54
D. 56

2.OA.1

10. The children brought in 37 leaves last week. Today they brought in 36 more. Which shows the total number of leaves?

A. 61   C. 71
B. 63   D. 73

2.OA.1

11. Which number sentence is shown using the model?

A. 3 + 3 = ?
B. 3 + 4 = ?
C. 3 + 3 + 3 + 3 = ?
D. 3 + 4 + 3 + 4 = ?

2.OA.4

12. Which number has 5 hundreds, 4 ones and 9 tens?

A. 495
B. 549
C. 594
D. 945

2.NBT.1

13. Which number has 8 tens and 6 ones and 0 hundreds?

A. 86
B. 608
C. 806
D. 860

4.NBT.1

14. Which is another way to show 100 ?

A. Ten ones
B. One ten
C. Ten tens
D. Ten hundreds

4.NBT.1a

15. Which shows the number three hundred seventy?

A. 37
B. 73
C. 307
D. 370

2.NBT.3

16. Which shows the number 400 + 3?

A. Forty-three
B. Forty-thirty
C. Four hundred three
D. Four hundred thirty

2.NBT.3

17. Which shows the number 9 ones 0 tens 2 hundreds?

A. 92
B. 209
C. 290
D. 902

2.NBT.1

18. Which symbol completes the number sentence?

Five hundred ninety six ? 596

A. <
B. >
C. =

2.NBT.4

19. Which number completes the number sentence?

$$812 > ?$$

A. 8 hundreds 2 ones
B. 8 hundreds 2 tens
C. 8 hundreds 1 ten 2 ones
D. 8 hundreds 1 ten 8 ones

2.NBT.4

20. Which set of numbers starts at 85 and skip counts by 5?

A. 85, 86, 87, 88
B. 85, 90, 95, 100,
C. 85, 95, 105, 115
D. 85, 100, 105, 110

2.NBT.2

21. Which set of numbers starts at 225 and skip counts by 10?

A. 225, 230, 235, 240
B. 225, 230, 240, 250
C. 225, 235, 245, 255
D. 225, 250, 275, 300

2.NBT.2

22. Which number completes the number sentence?

$$58 + ? = 88$$

A. 3
B. 30
C. 35
D. 38

2.OA.1

23. Which shows the sum of 26 + 6 + 12?

A. 32
B. 34
C. 44
D. 98

2.OA.1

24. Which number is 10 less than 741?

A. 641   C. 751
B. 731   D. 841

2.NBT.8

25. Which number is 100 more than 830?

A. 730
B. 820
C. 840
D. 930

2.NBT.8

Use the model below for questions 26-27

First Number

Second Number

Use the table below for questions 28-30
The table shows the number of stickers in each box.

Color	Red	Blue	Green	Yellow
Number of Stickers in Each Box	28	22	14	36

26. Which shows the sum of the first number and the second number?

A. 303
B. 313
C. 403
D. 413

2.NBT.7

27. Which shows the difference of the first number and the second number?

A. 33
B. 43
C. 133
D. 143

2.NBT.7

28. Which shows the total number of stickers for 1 red and 2 blue boxes?

A. 62
B. 68
C. 72
D. 78

2.NBT.6

29. Which shows the total number of stickers for 1 green and 2 yellow boxes?

A. 54
B. 64
C. 76
D. 86

2.NBT.6

30. Which shows the total number of stickers for 1 of each color box?

A. 64
B. 72
C. 90
D. 100

2.NBT.6

WEEK 11

ARGOPREP.COM

:: VIDEO ▶
EXPLANATIONS

This week we are measuring objects using a ruler. Lengths will be in inches and centimeters.

You can find detailed video explanations of each problem in the book by visiting:
ArgoPrep.com

1. Which shows the length of the paper clip?

A. 4 inches
B. 5 inches
C. 4 centimeters
D. 5 centimeters

2.MD.1

2. Which shows the length of the bow?

A. 5 feet
B. 5 inches
C. 5 meters
D. 5 centimeters

2.MD.1

3. Which shows the length of the pencil?

A. 16 feet
B. 16 inches
C. 16 meters
D. 16 centimeters

2.MD.1

4. Which shows the length of the phone?

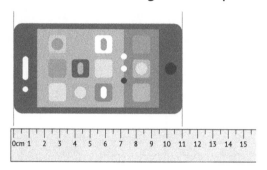

A. 11 feet
B. 11 inches
C. 11 meters
D. 11 centimeters

2.MD.1

5. Which shows the length of the bat?

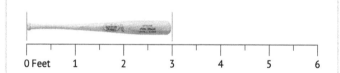

A. 3 feet
B. 3 inches
C. 3 meters
D. 3 centimeters

2.MD.1

TIP of the DAY

When measuring, be sure to check if the unit is inches (in) centimeters (cm) feet (ft) or meters (m). When the length is close or almost the measurement, we can use the closest length.

1. Each paper clip is 1 inch in length.

Which shows the length of the marker?

A. 4 inches   **C.** 4 centimeters

B. 5 inches   **D.** 5 centimeters

2.MD.2

2. Each pin is 1 centimeter in length.

Which shows the length of the crayon?

A. 6 inches   **C.** 6 centimeters

B. 7 inches   **D.** 7 centimeters

2.MD.2

3. Each part of the fence is 1 meter in length.

Which shows the length of the fence?

A. 6 feet   **C.** 6 meters

B. 7 feet   **D.** 7 meters

2.MD.2

4. Each ruler has a length of 1 foot.

How high is the window?

A. 4 feet

B. 5 feet

C. 4 meters

D. 5 meters

2.MD.1 & 2

5. Each pin has a length of 1 centimeter.

Which shows the length of the bow?

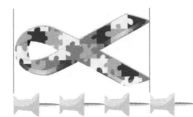

A. about 2 inches

B. about 3 inches

C. about 2 centimeters

D. about 3 centimeters

2.MD.3

TIP of the DAY

If we know the length of one thing, we can use it to measure other things.

1. The lengths of a key and some beads are shown.

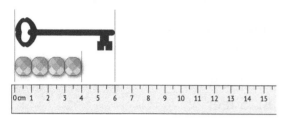

   Which sentence is true?

   A. The key is 2 centimeters longer than the beads.
   B. The key is 4 centimeters longer than the beads.
   C. The key is 6 centimeters longer than the beads.
   D. The key is 10 centimeters longer than the beads.

   2.MD.4

3. The lengths of a paintbrush and feather are shown.

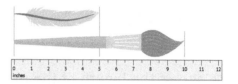

   Which sentence is true?

   A. The paintbrush is 5 inches longer than the feather.
   B. The paintbrush is 5 inches shorter than the feather.
   C. The feather is 5 centimeters longer than the paintbrush.
   D. The feather is 5 centimeters shorter than the paintbrush.

   2.MD.4

2. The lengths of a ribbon and a pen are shown.

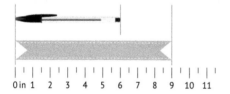

   Which sentence is true?

   A. The pen is 3 inches longer than the ribbon.
   B. The pen is 3 inches shorter than the ribbon.
   C. The ribbon is 3 centimeters longer than the pen.
   D. The ribbon is 3 centimeters shorter than the pen.

   2.MD.4

4. The lengths of a nail and a chain are shown.

   Which sentence is true?

   A. The chain is 10 inches longer than the nail.
   B. The chain is 10 inches shorter than the nail.
   C. The nail is 10 centimeters longer than the chain.
   D. The nail is 10 centimeters shorter than the chain.

   2.MD.4

TIP of the DAY

When comparing two lengths, count up or back from one to the other to find the difference.

WEEK 11 : DAY 4

1. Which could show the length of a book?

    A. 2 feet
    B. 12 inches
    C. 12 meters
    D. 2 centimeters

2.MD.3

4. Which could show the height of a child?

    A. 3 feet
    B. 3 inches
    C. 3 meters
    D. 3 centimeters

2.MD.3

2. Which could show the length of a car?

    A. 15 feet
    B. 15 inches
    C. 15 meters
    D. 15 centimeters

2.MD.3

5. Which could show the length of a banana?

    A. 9 feet
    B. 9 inches
    C. 9 meters
    D. 9 centimeters

2.MD.3

3. What could be a possible measurement of how high a room is?

    A. 3 feet
    B. 3 inches
    C. 3 meters
    D. 3 centimeters

2.MD.3

6. Which could show the length of a table?

    A. 2 feet
    B. 2 inches
    C. 10 centimeters
    D. 2 centimeters

2.MD.3

TIP of the DAY

We use inches and centimeters to measure smaller lengths. We use feet and meters to measure larger lengths.

1. Which shows the length of the tag?

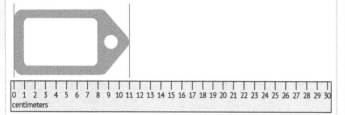

  A. 11 inches
  B. 12 inches
  C. 11 centimeters
  D. 12 centimeters

2.MD.1

2. The clip has a length of 1 inch.

Which shows the length of the eraser?

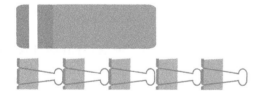

  A. 2 inches
  B. 3 inches
  C. 2 centimeters
  D. 3 centimeters

2.MD.2

3. The lengths of the spoon and straw are shown.

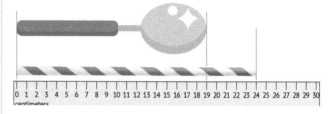

Which sentence is true?

  A. The straw is 5 cm longer than the spoon.
  B. The straw is 6 cm longer than the spoon.
  C. The straw is 19 cm longer than the spoon.
  D. The straw is 24 cm longer than the spoon.

2.MD.4

4. Which could show the height of a door?

  A. 8 feet   C. 8 meters
  B. 8 inches   D. 8 centimeters

2.MD.3

5. Which could show the length of a candy bar?

  A. 6 feet   C. 6 meters
  B. 6 inches   D. 6 centimeters

2.MD.3

DAY 6
Challenge question

A crayon has a length of 6 inches. How many crayons could have the same length as a table with a length of 3 feet, or 36 inches?
How did you find your answer?

WEEK 12

: VIDEO
EXPLANATIONS ▶

ARGOPREP.COM

This week we are solving problems using measurement.
Units will be inches, centimeters, feet and meters.

You can find detailed video explanations of each problem in the book by visiting:
ArgoPrep.com

WEEK 12 : DAY 1

1. The length of a crayon is 5 inches. The length of a crayon box is 7 inches longer. Which shows the length of the crayon box?

   A. 2 inches
   B. 5 inches
   C. 7 inches
   D. 12 inches

   2.MD.5

2. The length of a small ribbon is 14 inches. The length of a big ribbon is 22 inches. Which shows the total length of the two ribbons?

   A. 8 inches
   B. 14 inches
   C. 22 inches
   D. 36 inches

   2.MD.5

3. The length of a toy truck is 17 centimeters. The length of a toy car is 9 centimeters shorter. Which shows the length of the toy car?

   A. 8 centimeters
   B. 9 centimeters
   C. 17 centimeters
   D. 26 centimeters

   2.MD.5

4. A dog has a length of 29 inches. A cat has a length of 13 inches. Which shows how much longer the dog is than the cat?

   A. 13 inches
   B. 16 inches
   C. 29 inches
   D. 42 inches

   2.MD.5

5. The length of the sidewalk in front of Kim's house is 42 feet long. The length of the sidewalk next door to Kim's house is 28 feet long. Which shows the total length of both sidewalks?

   A. 14 feet   C. 42 feet
   B. 28 feet   D. 70 feet

   2.MD.5

6. Jen is 38 inches tall. Her sister is 55 inches tall. Which shows how many inches taller Jen's sister is than Jen?

   A. 17 inches
   B. 38 inches
   C. 55 inches
   D. 93 inches

   2.MD.5

TIP of the DAY

Use addition and subtraction to find the answers for questions about length.

84

1. The length of a book is 12 inches. This is 4 inches longer than the length of a bookmark. Which number sentence shows how to find the length of the bookmark?

   A. $12 - 2 = ?$ C. $12 + 2 = ?$
   B. $12 - 4 = ?$ D. $12 + 4 = ?$

   2.MD.5

2. The length of a red chain is 34 centimeters. The length of a green chain is 2 centimeters longer. Which number sentence shows how to find the total length of a red chain and a green chain?

   A. $34 + 2 = ?$ C. $34 + 36 = ?$
   B. $34 + 34 = ?$ D. $36 + 36 = ?$

   2.MD.5

3. There are two pictures on the wall. The length of one picture is 3 feet. The length of the other picture is 1 foot longer than the first picture. Which number sentence shows how to find the length of the longer picture?

   A. $3 + 1 = ?$ C. $4 - 3 = ?$
   B. $3 - 1 = ?$ D. $4 + 3 = ?$

   2.MD.5

Use the table for questions 4-6.

The table shows the length of some toy trains.

Train Color	Red	Blue	Green
Length in inches	14	16	15

4. Which shows the total number of inches of 1 red and 1 blue train?

   A. 20
   B. 28
   C. 30
   D. 32

   2.MD.5

5. Which shows the total number of inches of 1 blue and 1 green train?

   A. 30
   B. 31
   C. 32
   D. 45

   2.MD.5

6. Which shows the total number of inches for 1 red, 1 blue and 1 green train?

   A. 35
   B. 42
   C. 45
   D. 48

   2.MD.5

TIP of the DAY

When writing number sentences, read the question carefully to think about whether to add or subtract.

Use the table below for questions 1-6

Tile Color	White	Black	Yellow	Orange
Length in Centimeters	12	16	15	14

Nick is putting some color tiles together. When he puts them together he wants to find the total length of the tiles.

1. Which shows the total length, in centimeters, of 2 white and 2 black tiles?

   A. 24   C. 48
   B. 32   D. 56

   2.MD.5

2. Which shows the total length, in centimeters, of 2 black and 2 orange tiles?

   A. 30   C. 60
   B. 56   D. 64

   2.MD.5

3. Which shows the total length, in centimeters, of 1 tile of each color?

   A. 57
   B. 60
   C. 64
   D. 67

   2.MD.5

4. Which shows how many centimeters longer 3 black tiles are than 3 orange tiles?

   A. 2
   B. 3
   C. 4
   D. 6

   2.MD.5

5. Which shows how many centimeters longer 2 orange tiles are than 1 yellow tile?

   A. 13
   B. 28
   C. 43
   D. 58

   2.MD.5

6. Which shows the correct order of the color tiles, from shortest to longest in length?

   A. White, Black, Yellow, Orange
   B. White, Orange, Yellow, Black
   C. Black, Yellow, Orange, White
   D. Black, White, Orange, Yellow

   2.MD.5

TIP of the DAY

The length is how long something is. We can put lengths together to find the total length.

1. Kim has 2 pictures. Each picture has a length of 6 inches. Which shows the total length of the 2 pictures?

   A. 8 inches
   B. 10 inches
   C. 12 inches
   D. 14 inches

   2.MD.5

2. Maya's book has a length of 18 centimeters. Her bookmark has a length of 13 centimeters. Which shows how much longer the book is than the bookmark?

   A. 5 centimeters
   B. 13 centimeters
   C. 21 centimeters
   D. 31 centimeters

   2.MD.5

3. The wall in front of a house has a length of 24 feet. The wall in the back of the house has a length of 41 feet. Which shows the total length of both walls?

   A. 17 feet
   B. 27 feet
   C. 65 feet
   D. 75 feet

   2.MD.5

4. Vin wants to put 3 desks together. Each desk has a length of 26 inches. Which shows the total length of the 3 desks?

   A. 29 inches
   B. 32 inches
   C. 68 inches
   D. 78 inches

   2.MD.5

5. There are 2 trays on the table. The small tray has a length of 18 centimeters. The large tray has a length of 36 centimeters. Which shows the total length of the 2 trays?

   A. 36 centimeters
   B. 54 centimeters
   C. 58 centimeters
   D. 72 centimeters

   2.MD.5

6. There are 2 flags on the wall. Each flag has a length of 20 inches. The length between the flags is 6 inches.

   Which shows the total length of the 2 flags and the length in between on the wall?

   A. 26 inches
   B. 28 inches
   C. 40 inches
   D. 46 inches

   2.MD.5

TIP of the DAY

If the question asks what the length is and does not include the unit of measurement (inches, centimeters, feet, meters) then the answer should include the measurement.
What is the length in inches?   4
What is the length?   4 inches

Use the picture for #1-6

Ben's shoe has a length of 19 centimeters. His brother's shoe is 5 centimeters longer.

19 centimeters

1. Which number sentence shows how to find the length of Ben's brother's shoe?

A. 19 − 5 = ?
C. 19 + 5 = ?
B. 19 − 14 = ?
D. 19 + 14 = ?

2.MD.5

2. Which number sentence shows how to find the total length of 1 of Ben's shoes and 1 of his brother's shoes?

A. 19 + 5 = ?
C. 19 + 19 = ?
B. 19 + 14 = ?
D. 19 + 24 = ?

2.MD.5

3. Which shows the total length of 2 of Ben's shoes?

A. 38 inches
C. 48 inches
B. 38 centimeters
D. 48 centimeters

2.MD.5

4. Which shows the total length of 2 of Ben's brother's shoes?

A. 38 inches
B. 38 centimeters
C. 48 inches
D. 48 centimeters

2.MD.5

5. Ben has a pair of new shoes. Since he has grown, his new shoes are 3 centimeters longer. Which shows the length of one of Ben's new shoes?

A. 16 centimeters
B. 22 centimeters
C. 24 centimeters
D. 27 centimeters

2.MD.5

6. Which shows the length of 2 of Ben's new shoes?

A. 24 centimeters
B. 25 centimeters
C. 44 centimeters
D. 48 centimeters

2.MD.5

DAY 6
Challenge question

The square has 4 sides. The length of each side is 5 centimeters
What is the total length of the 4 sides of the square?

5 centimeters

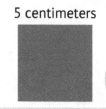

WEEK 13

ARGOPREP.COM

: VIDEO
EXPLANATIONS ▶

This week we are using number lines and number charts to find missing numbers.
Numbers will go up to 100.

You can find detailed video explanations of each problem in the book by visiting:
ArgoPrep.com

1. A number line is shown.

Which shows the missing number?

A. 4
B. 7
C. 10
D. 11

2.MD.6

2. A number line is shown.

Which shows the missing number?

A. 15
B. 19
C. 21
D. 22

2.MD.6

3. A number chart is shown.

| 46 | 47 | ? | 49 | 50 |

Which shows the missing number?

A. 40   C. 48
B. 45   D. 51

2.MD.6

4. A number chart is shown.

| 6 | ? | 8 | 9 | ? |

Which two numbers complete the chart?

A. 5 and 7
B. 5 and 10
C. 7 and 10
D. 7 and 11

2.MD.6

5. A number chart is shown.

| 23 | 22 | 21 | 20 | ? |

Which shows the missing number?

A. 19   C. 24
B. 21   D. 25

2.MD.6

TIP of the DAY

When finding missing numbers on a number line or a number chart, count the numbers that you see and look for a pattern.

WEEK 13 : DAY 2

1. A number pattern is shown.

5	7	9	?

Which shows the missing number?

A. 4   **C.** 10
B. 8   **D.** 11

2.MD.6

2. A number pattern is shown.

38	36	34	32	?

Which shows the fifth number?

A. 30
B. 31
C. 39
D. 40

2.MD.6

3. A number pattern is shown.

15	20	25	30	?

Which shows the fifth number?

A. 10
B. 31
C. 35
D. 40

2.MD.6

4. A number pattern is shown.

3   13   ◯   33

Which shows the third number?

A. 14
B. 15
C. 23
D. 32

2.MD.6

5. A number pattern is shown.

70   68   66   ?

Which shows the missing number?

A. 60
B. 64
C. 65
D. 67

2.MD.6

TIP
of the
DAY

When finding the missing number, find how much the number pattern is counting up or down by and how the pattern would keep going.

WEEK 13 : DAY 3

1. A number chart is shown.

14	15
?	25

Which shows the missing number?

A. 12

B. 16

C. 24

D. 26

2.MD.6

2. A number chart is shown.

?	63
72	?

Which shows the pair of missing numbers?

A. 62 and 72

B. 63 and 73

C. 64 and 71

D. 62 and 73

2.MD.6

3. A number chart is shown.

21	22	?
31	32	33
?	42	43

Which shows the pair of missing numbers?

A. 23 and 24

B. 23 and 30

C. 23 and 41

D. 23 and 44

2.MD.6

4. A number chart is shown.

78	77	76
68	?	66
58	57	?

Which shows the pair of missing numbers?

A. 65 and 56

B. 67 and 56

C. 69 and 58

D. 87 and 76

2.MD.6

5. A number chart is shown.

34	36	38	40
?	46	48	?
54	56	58	60

Which shows the pair of missing numbers?

A. 41 and 49

B. 42 and 50

C. 44 and 49

D. 44 and 50

2.MD.6

TIP of the DAY

Sometimes we look to number charts to find missing numbers. Think about the numbers around the missing number and look for patterns to help.

7	8	9
17	?	19
27	28	29

Counting by 1's across

Counting by 10's down

92

WEEK 13 : DAY 4

1. Rob was 39 inches tall. Then he grew. Now he is 48 inches tall. Which shows how many inches Rob grew?

   A. 1
   B. 8
   C. 9
   D. 11

   2.MD.6

2. Lisa has a plant that is 12 centimeters high. Last month it was 8 centimeters high. Which shows how many centimeters the plant grew?

   A. 4
   B. 8
   C. 12
   D. 20

   2.MD.6

3. A table is 3 feet high. On top of the table is a box that is 2 feet high. Which shows the height, the total number of feet, for the table and the box?

   A. 1
   B. 2
   C. 3
   D. 5

   2.MD.6

4. Jake is standing on a chair that is 24 inches high. Jake is 40 inches tall. While standing on the chair, he is now as tall as his sister.

   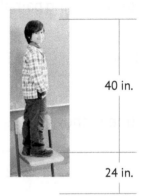

   Which shows how many inches tall Jake's sister is?

   A. 16   C. 40
   B. 24   D. 64

   2.MD.6

5. There are 3 blocks as shown. Each block is 4 inches high. Which shows the height, the total number of inches, of the three blocks?

   A. 3
   B. 4
   C. 7
   D. 12

   2.MD.6

TIP of the DAY

When we measure how tall something is, it is like measuring length but up and down instead of across.

WEEK 13 : DAY 5

1. A number line is shown.

15   14   ?   ?   11   10

Which shows the missing pair of numbers?

A. 13 and 12   **C.** 15 and 12
B. 13 and 14   **D.** 15 and 16

2.MD.6

2. A number line is shown.

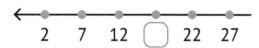

2   7   12   ⬚   22   27

Which shows the missing number?

A. 13   **C.** 17
B. 14   **D.** 21

2.MD.6

3. A number chart is shown.

28	30	?
38	40	42
48	?	52

Which shows the pair of missing numbers?

A. 31 and 49   **C.** 31 and 50
B. 32 and 51   **D.** 32 and 50

2.MD.6

4. The diagram below shows 2 windows. The length of each window is 18 inches.

18 in.   18 in.

Which shows the total length, in inches, of the 2 windows?

A. 18   **D.** 38
B. 20
C. 36

2.MD.6

5. Deb is 88 centimeters tall. She is 9 centimeters taller than her sister. Which shows the height, in centimeters, of her sister?

A. 79
B. 81
C. 89
D. 97

2.MD.6

DAY 6
Challenge question

A plant has a height of 22 centimeters. If the plant grows 3 centimeters each week, what would the height of the plant be 4 weeks from now?

WEEK 14

ARGOPREP.COM

VIDEO
EXPLANATIONS

This week we are telling and writing time using clocks. We will use time on an analog clock.

You can find detailed video explanations of each problem in the book by visiting:
ArgoPrep.com

1. Which time is shown on the clock?

A. 8:00   **C.** 12:08
B. 8:12   **D.** 12:40

2.MD.7

2. Which time is shown on the clock?

A. 2:06   **C.** 6:02
B. 2:30   **D.** 6:10

2.MD.7

3. Which time is shown on the clock?

A. 3:07   **C.** 7:03
B. 3:35   **D.** 7:15

2.MD.7

4. Which time is shown on the clock?

A. 1:09
B. 1:45
C. 9:01
D. 9:05

2.MD.7

5. Which time is shown on the clock?

A. 1:03
B. 1:15
C. 2:03
D. 2:15

2.MD.7

TIP of the DAY

When telling time, the big hand shows the hour and the small hand shows the minutes.

1. Which time is shown on the clock?

A. 2:07 C. 7:02

B. 2:35 D. 7:10

2.MD.7

2. Which time is shown on the clock?

A. 1:08 C. 8:01

B. 1:40 D. 8:05

2.MD.7

3. Which time is shown on the clock?

A. 2:04 C. 4:02

B. 2:20 D. 4:10

2.MD.7

4. Which time is shown on the clock?

A. 1:09

B. 1:45

C. 12:09

D. 12:45

2.MD.7

5. Which time is shown on the clock?

A. 10:11

B. 10:50

C. 11:10

D. 11:50

2.MD.7

TIP of the DAY

On a clock you see the numbers 1-12. Sometimes you can see tic marks in between the numbers. Each tic mark is 1 minute. As the minute hand moves, count by 5 minutes as it moves to the next number.

3:00

3:05

The time on this clock is 3:00. The minute hand is on the 12. When the minute hand moves from the 12 to 1, 5 minutes have passed.

1. Which time is shown on the clock?

A. 2 minutes after 6
B. 10 minutes after 6
C. 6 minutes after 2
D. 6 minutes after 10

2.MD.7

2. Which time is shown on the clock?

A. 1 minute after 11
B. 5 minutes after 11
C. 11 minutes before 1
D. 11 minutes before 5

2.MD.7

3. Which time is shown on the clock?

A. 7 minutes to 8
B. 7 minutes after 7
C. 20 minutes to 7
D. 25 minutes after 8

2.MD.7

4. Which time is shown on the clock?

A. 5 minutes to 5
B. 5 minutes after 11
C. 11 minutes to 5
D. 11 minutes after 11

2.MD.7

5. Which time is shown on the clock?

A. 8 minutes to 9
B. 9 minutes to 8
C. 15 minutes to 8
D. 20 minutes to 9

2.MD.7

TIP of the DAY

Another way to tell time is to tell the minutes after the hour that has just passed and the number of minutes to the next hour.

3:15 is also 15 minutes after 3

3:45 is 45 minutes after 3 or 15 minutes to 4.

1. Mark ate his breakfast at the time shown.

Which shows the time that Mark ate his breakfast?

A. 7:30 a.m.   C. 8:30 a.m.
B. 7:30 p.m.   D. 8:30 p.m.

2.MD.7

2. After school, Jan did her homework at the time shown.

Which shows the time that Jan did her homework?

A. 3:30 a.m.   C. 4:30 a.m.
B. 3:30 p.m.   D. 4:30 p.m.

2.MD.7

3. At 9:00 p.m. which would children be most likely doing?
   A. Eating breakfast
   B. Sitting at their desks in school
   C. Eating dinner
   D. Getting ready to go to sleep   2.MD.7

4. At 10:00 a.m., which would children be most likely doing?
   A. Waking up from sleeping
   B. Sitting in their desks in school
   C. Going home after school
   D. Getting ready to go to sleep   2.MD.7

5. At 12:00 noon, which would children be most likely doing?
   A. Going to school
   B. Eating lunch
   C. Going home from school
   D. Sleeping in their beds   2.MD.7

6. At 12:00 midnight, which would children be most likely doing?
   A. Going to school
   B. Eating lunch
   C. Going home from school
   D. Sleeping in their beds   2.MD.7

TIP of the DAY

The times are repeated 2 times each day. The a.m. times are for the first part of the day (from 12:00 midnight until 12:00 noon). The p.m. times are for the second part of the day (from 12:00 noon until 12:00 midnight).
Think about a.m. as early in the morning until lunch time and p.m. from lunch time until late night.

WEEK 14 : DAY 5

ASSESSMENT

1. Kris ate dinner at the time shown.

Which shows the time that Kris ate dinner?

A. 5:00 a.m.   C. 12:05 a.m.
B. 5:00 p.m.   D. 12:05 p.m.

2.MD.7

2. Which time is shown on the clock?

A. 9:06
B. 9:30
C. 10:06
D. 10:30

2.MD.7

3. Which time is shown on the clock?

A. 4:00
B. 4:12
C. 12:04
D. 12:20

2.MD.7

4. Which time is shown on the clock?

A. 9 minutes to 12
B. 12 minutes to 9
C. 15 minutes to 11
D. 15 minutes to 12

2.MD.7

5. Which time is shown on the clock?

A. 1 minute after 6
B. 6 minutes after 1
C. 30 minutes after 1
D. 30 minutes after 2

2.MD.7

DAY 6
Challenge question

Place the times shown on the clocks:
A. 7:00
B. 11:30
C. 9:15
D. 4:45

100

WEEK 15

This week we are counting money. This includes dollars, quarters, dimes, nickels and pennies.

You can find detailed video explanations of each problem in the book by visiting:
ArgoPrep.com

WEEK 15 : DAY 1

1. Which shows the total amount of 4 pennies?

- A. 1¢
- B. 4¢
- C. 5¢
- D. 14¢

2.MD.8

2. Which shows the total amount of 3 nickels?

- A. 3¢
- B. 13¢
- C. 15¢
- D. 30¢

2.MD.8

3. Which shows the total amount of 4 dimes?

- A. 4¢
- B. 14¢
- C. 20¢
- D. 40¢

2.MD.8

4. Which shows the total amount of 3 quarters?

- A. 3¢
- B. 15¢
- C. 30¢
- D. 75¢

2.MD.8

5. Which shows the amount of 7 nickels?

- A. 7¢
- B. 17¢
- C. 35¢
- D. 70¢

2.MD.8

6. Which shows the amount of 9 dollar bills?

- A. 9¢
- B. 90¢
- C. $9
- D. $90

2.MD.8

TIP *of the* DAY

When counting money, the coins we use are pennies, nickels, dimes and quarters. We can use bills like the one dollar bill. The coins and bills and the amounts are shown.

penny	nickel	dime	quarter	one dollar
1¢	5¢	10¢	25¢	$1.00
one cent	five cents	ten cents	twenty-five cents	one hundred cents

WEEK 15 : DAY 2

1. Which shows the amount equal to 15¢?

  A. 5 pennies and 1 nickel
  B. 5 pennies and 1 dime
  C. 5 pennies and 2 dimes
  D. 5 pennies and 5 nickels

4. Which shows the amount equal to 80¢?

  A. 3 quarters 1 dime and 1 nickel
  B. 2 quarters 1 dime and 2 nickels
  C. 2 quarters 2 dimes and 3 nickels
  D. 2 quarters 2 dimes and 2 nickels

2. Which shows the amount equal to 25¢?

  A. 2 dimes and 2 nickels
  B. 2 dimes and 5 nickels
  C. 1 dime and 15 pennies
  D. 1 dime and 25 pennies

5. Which shows the amount equal to $1.00?

  A. 3 quarters 1 dime and 1 nickel
  B. 3 quarters 2 dimes and 1 nickel
  C. 3 quarters 2 dimes and 2 nickels
  D. 3 quarters 3 dimes and 1 nickel

3. Which shows the amount equal to 50¢?

  A. 3 dimes 3 nickels and 5 pennies
  B. 2 dimes 4 nickels and 5 pennies
  C. 3 dimes 4 nickels and 5 pennies
  D. 4 dimes 2 nickels and 5 pennies

6. Which shows the amount equal to $1.00?

  A. 2 quarters 3 dimes and 1 nickel
  B. 2 quarters 4 dimes and 1 nickel
  C. 2 quarters 4 dimes and 2 nickels
  D. 2 quarters 5 dimes and 2 nickels

TIP of the DAY

We can use different amount of coins to show the same amount.
5 pennies = 1 nickel, 2 nickels = 1 dime, 5 nickels = 1 quarter
2 dimes and 1 nickel = 1 quarter
4 quarters or 10 dimes or 20 nickels or
100 pennies = 1 dollar

1. Which shows the total amount of money?

A. $2.44
B. $2.74
C. $2.84
D. $2.94

2.MD.8

2. Which shows the total amount of money?

A. $1.88
B. $1.93
C. $2.03
D. $2.18

2.MD.8

3. Which shows the total amount of money?

A. $2.46   C. $2.71
B. $2.51   D. $2.96   2.MD.8

4. Which shows the total amount of money?

A. $3.71   C. $4.06
B. $4.05   D. $4.35   2.MD.8

5. Which shows the total amount of money?

A. $2.52   C. $3.52
B. $3.32   D. $4.12   2.MD.8

When finding the amount of money of dollars and coins, find all the amounts of each and add the amounts together.

1 dollar bill + 1 quarter + 3 nickels + 6 pennies
$1.00 + 25¢ + 15¢ + 6¢= $1.46

TIP
of the
DAY

1. Which shows 45¢ using the least number of coins?

   A. 9 nickels
   B. 4 dimes and 1 nickel
   C. 1 quarter and 2 dimes
   D. 1 quarter 1 dime and 2 nickels

   2.MD.8

2. Which shows 68¢ using the least number of coins?

   A. 6 dimes and 8 pennies
   B. 6 dimes 1 nickel and 3 pennies
   C. 2 quarters 1 dime and 8 pennies
   D. 2 quarters 1 dime 1 nickel and 3 pennies

   2.MD.8

3. Which shows 99¢ using the least number of coins?

   A. 9 dimes and 9 pennies
   B. 2 quarters 4 dimes and 9 pennies
   C. 3 quarters 2 dimes and 4 pennies
   D. 3 quarters 1 dime 2 nickels and 4 pennies

   2.MD.8

4. Which shows $1.35 using the least number of bills and coins?

   A. 1 dollar bill 1 quarter 1 dime
   B. 1 dollar bill 1 dime and 5 nickels
   C. 1 dollar bill 2 dimes and 3 nickels
   D. 1 dollar bill 1 quarter and 2 nickels

   2.MD.8

5. Which shows $2.12 using the least number of bills and coins?

   A. 2 dollar bills and 12 pennies
   B. 2 dollar bills 1 dime and 2 pennies
   C. 2 dollar bills 1 nickel and 7 pennies
   D. 2 dollar bills 2 nickels and 2 pennies

   2.MD.8

TIP of the DAY

When buying something, we sometimes try to use the largest coins possible so that we can use the least number of bills and coins.
For 30¢, you can use 3 dimes (3 coins) or 1 quarter and 1 nickel (2 coins)
For 85¢, you can use 8 dimes and 1 nickel (9 coins) or 3 quarters and 1 dime (4 coins)

1. Which shows the amount of 5 quarters?

   A. 5¢
   B. 25¢
   C. 50¢
   D. $1.25

   2.MD.8

2. Which shows the amount equal to 75¢?

   A. 7 dimes and 3 nickels
   B. 1 quarter 5 dimes and 1 nickel
   C. 5 dimes 4 nickels and 5 pennies
   D. 4 dimes 7 nickels and 5 pennies

   2.MD.8

3. Which shows the total amount of money?

   A. $3.86
   B. $4.76
   C. $4.91
   D. $5.01

   2.MD.8

4. Which shows $1.58 using the least number of coins?

   A. 1 dollar bill 5 dimes and 8 pennies
   B. 1 dollar bill 2 quarters and 8 pennies
   C. 1 dollar bill 2 quarters 1 nickel and 3 pennies
   D. 1 dollar bill 1 quarter 3 dimes 1 nickel and 3 pennies

   2.MD.8

5. Which shows $3.33 using the least number of coins?

   A. 3 dollar bills 3 dimes and 3 pennies
   B. 3 dollar bills 1 quarter and 8 pennies
   C. 3 dollar bills 1 dime 3 nickels and 8 pennies
   D. 3 dollar bills 1 quarter 1 nickel and 3 pennies

   2.MD.8

DAY 6
Challenge question

Mike has 88¢ in his pocket. He has exactly 9 coins. What are the coins that Mike has in his pocket?

106

ARGOPREP.COM

VIDEO
EXPLANATIONS

This week we are solving problems using line plots.
We will use addition and subtraction to problem solve.

You can find detailed video explanations of each problem in the book by visiting:
ArgoPrep.com

Use the Line Plot for questions 1-5.

Number of Boxes with Different Amounts of Toys

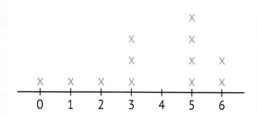

Number of Toys in a Box

The children found some boxes. In some of the boxes there were different amounts of toys. The Xs show how many boxes had each number of toys.

2.MD.9

1. In how many boxes were there 5 toys?

   A. 3
   B. 4
   C. 5
   D. 6

   2.MD.9

2. In how many boxes were there 0 toys?

   A. 0
   B. 1
   C. 2
   D. 3

   2.MD.9

3. There were no boxes with this amount of toys. Which amount was that?

   A. 3
   B. 4
   C. 5
   D. 6

   2.MD.9

4. Which box contains the greatest amount of toys?

   A. 3
   B. 4
   C. 5
   D. 6

   2.MD.9

5. Which statement is true?

   A. There were 3 boxes with 3 toys.
   B. There were 2 boxes with 2 toys.
   C. There were 4 boxes with 3 toys.
   D. All boxes had at least 1 toy inside.

   2.MD.9

TIP of the DAY

A line plot can be used to show the number of different amounts. For example in the line plot above, there are boxes with 0 toys, 1 toy, 2 toys, 3 toys, 4 toys, 5 toys and 6 toys. The X's tell us how many boxes had each amount of toys.

Use the line plot for questions 1-5.

Number of Students Taking Music Lessons

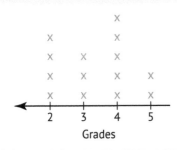

The line plot shows the number of students in grades 2-5 who are taking music lessons.

2.MD.9

1. Which shows the number of students in grade 2 that are taking lessons?

A. 2
B. 3
C. 4
D. 5

2.MD.9

2. In which grade are there 2 students taking lessons?

A. 2
B. 3
C. 4
D. 5

2.MD.9

3. In which grade are the most number of students taking lessons?

A. 2
B. 3
C. 4
D. 5

2.MD.9

4. In which grade are the least number of students taking lessons?

A. 2
B. 3
C. 4
D. 5

2.MD.9

5. Which shows the number of students in grade 3 that are taking lessons?

A. 2
B. 3
C. 4
D. 5

2.MD.9

TIP
of the
DAY

Make sure you check the titles of the line plot to understand what the amounts are and what is being counted.

109

Use the line plot for questions 1-5.

Number of Pumpkins and What they Cost

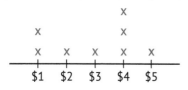

Cost of the Pumpkins

There are pumpkins of different sizes for sale. The number of pumpkins that cost between $1 and $5 are shown on the line plot.

2.MD.9

3. Which shows the number of pumpkins being sold for $1?

A. 1
B. 2
C. 3
D. 4

2.MD.9

1. Which shows the number of pumpkins being sold for $5?

A. 1
B. 2
C. 3
D. 5

2.MD.9

4. There are 3 pumpkins being sold for the same cost. Which shows the cost?

A. $2
B. $3
C. $4
D. $5

2.MD.9

2. Which shows the number of pumpkins being sold for $4

A. 1
B. 2
C. 3
D. 4

2.MD.9

5. Which shows the total amount of pumpkins that are being sold?

A. 5
B. 6
C. 7
D. 8

2.MD.9

TIP
of the
DAY

If you count all of the X's you will know the total number of items in the line plot.

Use the line plot for questions 1-5.
The lengths of some leaves were measured. The line plots show the number of leaves for each measurement.

Number of Leaves for Each Length

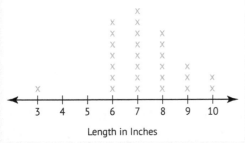

Length in Inches

2.MD.9

1. Which shows the number of leaves that measured 6 inches?

A. 6
B. 7
C. 8
D. 9

2.MD.9

2. Which shows the number of leaves that measured 5 inches?

A. 0
B. 1
C. 2
D. 3

2.MD.9

3. There are 3 leaves with the same measurement. Which shows the length of the 3 leaves?

A. 7
B. 8
C. 9
D. 10

2.MD.9

4. One more leaf was measured and added to the line plot. The leaf measured 10 inches. Which shows the new number of leaves that measured 10 inches?

A. 2
B. 3
C. 4
D. 5

2.MD.9

5. One more leaf was measured and added to the line plot. The leaf measured 5 inches. Which shows the new number of leaves that measured 5 inches?

A. 0
B. 1
C. 2
D. 3

2.MD.9

TIP of the DAY

When adding to the line plot, carefully look where the new X will be placed.

WEEK 16 : DAY 5

Use the line plot for questions 1-5.

Number of Classes

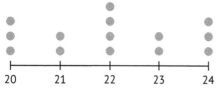

Number of Students in the Class

There are classes with student totals between 20 and 24. The line plot shows the classes that have each number of students.

2.MD.9

1. Which shows the number of classes with 24 students?

   A. 2
   B. 3
   C. 4
   D. 5

2.MD.9

2. There are 4 classes with the same number of students. Which shows the number of students in the classes?

   A. 21   C. 23
   B. 22   D. 24

2.MD.9

3. Which shows the total number of classes?

   A. 14
   B. 15
   C. 16
   D. 17

2.MD.9

4. One of the classes that had 20 students now has 1 more student. Which shows the new number of classes that now have 20 students?

   A. 1
   B. 2
   C. 3
   D. 4

2.MD.9

5. Which shows the number of classes with the greatest number of students?

   A. 1
   B. 2
   C. 3
   D. 4

2.MD.9

DAY 6
Challenge question

The table shows the ages of some children that play board games after school. Ages of Children Playing Board Games

7	8	8	7	9	8	9	10	8	10

Make a Line Plot to show the number of children for each age.

Number of Children Playing Board Games

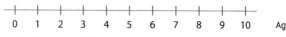

WEEK 17

This week we are solving problems using pictograms and bar models. We will use addition and subtraction to problem solve.

You can find detailed video explanations of each problem in the book by visiting:
ArgoPrep.com

Use the pictograph for questions 1-5.

House	Number of Trees
Brown	🌳🌳🌳
Blue	🌳🌳🌳🌳🌳🌳
Green	🌳🌳
White	🌳🌳🌳🌳

Key: 🌳 = 1 Tree

The children counted the number of trees in the back of 4 houses. The pictograph shows the number of trees for each house.

1. Which shows the number of trees in the back of the green house?

A. 2
B. 3
C. 4
D. 6

2.MD.10

2. Which house has the greatest number of trees?

A. Brown
B. Blue
C. Green
D. White

2.MD.10

3. Which shows the number of trees in the back of the brown house?

A. 2
B. 3
C. 4
D. 6

2.MD.10

4. Which house has the least number of trees?

A. Brown
B. Blue
C. Green
D. White

2.MD.10

5. Which shows the number of trees in the back of the white house?

A. 2
B. 3
C. 4
D. 6

2.MD.10

When reading a pictograph, be sure to check the key to see what one picture is equal to.

114

Use the pictograph for questions 1-5.

Box	Number of Pencils
Red	/ / / /
Yellow	/ / / / / / / / / /
Black	/ / / / / /
Blue	/ / / / / / / /

Key: / = 1 Pencil

The students counted the number of pencils in 4 different color boxes. The pictograph shows the number of pencils in each box.

1. Which shows the number of pencils in the yellow box?

A. 4   C. 8
B. 6   D. 10

2.MD.10

2. Which box has the least number of pencils?

A. red
B. yellow
C. black
D. blue

2.MD.10

3. Which shows the total number of pencils in the red and yellow boxes?

A. 4
B. 6
C. 10
D. 14

2.MD.10

4. Which shows the total number of pencils in the black and blue boxes?

A. 2
B. 6
C. 8
D. 14

2.MD.10

5. Which shows how many more pencils are in the yellow box than the black box?

A. 4
B. 6
C. 10
D. 14

2.MD.10

TIP
of the
DAY

Carefully read the pictograph when adding and subtracting the numbers that show the amounts.

115

Use the bar graph below for questions 1-5.

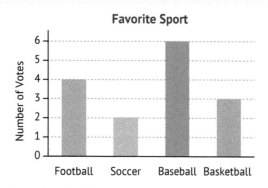

Favorite Sport

The students voted on their favorite sport to play. The bar graph shows the number of students that voted for each sport.

2.MD.10

1. Which shows the number of votes for Soccer?

A. 2
B. 3
C. 4
D. 6

2.MD.10

2. Which sport had 3 votes?

A. Football
B. Soccer
C. Baseball
D. Basketball

2.MD.10

3. Which shows the number of votes for Football?

A. 2
B. 3
C. 4
D. 6

2.MD.10

4. Which sport has the greatest number of votes?

A. Football
B. Soccer
C. Baseball
D. Basketball

2.MD.10

5. Which sport has the least number of votes?

A. Football
B. Soccer
C. Baseball
D. Basketball

2.MD.10

TIP of the DAY

When reading a bar graph, be sure to look across from the number to see the bar height and then look down to see what is being measured.

116

Use the Bar Graph below for questions 1-5. The students made a bar graph to show their birthdays in each season.

Number of Birthdays in Each Season

2.MD.10

1. Which shows the number of students with Fall birthdays?

A. 8   C. 10
B. 6   D. 1

2.MD.10

2. Which shows the season with 6 students who have birthdays?

A. Fall   C. Spring
B. Winter   D. Summer

2.MD.10

3. Which shows the total number of students with birthdays in Winter and Spring?

A. 6
B. 10
C. 14
D. 16

2.MD.10

4. Which shows the total number of students with birthdays in Spring and Summer?

A. 1
B. 10
C. 11
D. 16

2.MD.10

5. Which shows how many more students have birthdays in Spring than in Fall?

A. 2
B. 8
C. 10
D. 12

2.MD.10

TIP of the DAY

When using the bar graph to add and subtract the bar heights, write the heights down and then add or subtract.

WEEK 17 : DAY 5

Use the bar graph for questions 1-5.
The bar graph shows the number of students and their folder color

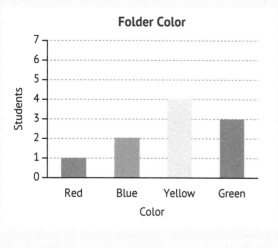

Folder Color

1. Which shows the number of students that have green folders?

   A. 1   C. 3
   B. 2   D. 4

   2.MD.10

2. Which shows the folder color that the greatest number of students has?

   A. Red
   B. Blue
   C. Yellow
   D. Green

   2.MD.10

3. Which shows how many more students have yellow folders than red folders?

   A. 1
   B. 2
   C. 3
   D. 4

   2.MD.10

4. Which shows the folder color that the least number of students has?

   A. Red
   B. Blue
   C. Yellow
   D. Green

   2.MD.10

5. Which shows the total number of folders?

   A. 4
   B. 6
   C. 8
   D. 10

   2.MD.10

DAY 6
Challenge question

Write a question for the bar graph from Day 5.

118

WEEK 18

ARGOPREP.COM

VIDEO
EXPLANATIONS ▶

This week we are counting the number of sides and angles in shapes. We will use shapes from 3 sides to 6 sides.

You can find detailed video explanations of each problem in the book by visiting: ArgoPrep.com

WEEK 18 : DAY 1

1. How many sides does the figure below have?

A. 2
B. 3
C. 4
D. 5

2.G.1

2. Which shape is made up of straight sides?

A.

B.

C.

D.

2.G.1

3. Which shape has 4 sides?

A.

B.

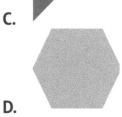
C.

D.

2.G.1

4. A shape is shown below.

Which shows the number of sides?

A. 4
B. 5
C. 6
D. 7

2.G.1

TIP of the DAY

Flat shapes have straight sides that we can count.

120

1. A shape is shown below.

Which shows the number of angles?

A. 2
B. 3
C. 4
D. 5

2.G.1

2. A shape is shown below.

Which statement is true?

A. The shape has 6 sides and 4 angles.
B. The shape has 4 sides and 4 angles.
C. The shape has 4 sides and 6 angles.
D. The shape has 6 sides and 6 angles.

2.G.1

3. Which shape has 4 angles?

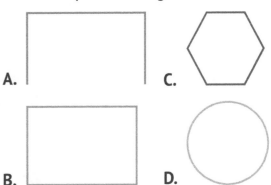

A.   **C.**
B.   **D.**

2.G.1

4. A shape is shown below.

Which shows the number of sides?

A. 3   **C.** 5
B. 4   **D.** 6

2.G.1

5. Which shows the number of angles that a 6 sided shape has?

A. 3
B. 4
C. 5
D. 6

2.G.1

TIP of the DAY

Shapes that are made of straight sides have angles where the sides bend. The number of angles are the same as the number of sides.

WEEK 18 : DAY 3

1. Which shape does NOT have 3 sides?

A.

C.

B.

D.

2.G.1

3. Which shape does NOT have 5 sides?

A.

C.

B.

D.

2.G.1

2. Which shape does NOT have 4 sides?

A.

C.

B.

D.

2.G.1

4. Which shape does NOT has 6 sides?

A.

C.

B.

D.

2.G.1

TIP of the DAY

Be careful with questions that ask NOT.

122

WEEK 18 : DAY 4

1. Two shapes are shown.

Which shows the total number of sides for both shapes?

A. 4   **B.** 6   **C.** 7   **D.** 8

2.G.1

2. Two shapes are shown.

Which shows the total number of sides for both shapes?

A. 8   **B.** 9   **C.** 10   **D.** 11

2.G.1

3. Two shapes are shown.

Which statement is true?

Shape 1   Shape 2

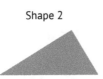

A. Shape 1 has 3 more sides than Shape 2
B. Shape 2 has 3 more sides than Shape 1
C. Shape 1 has 4 more sides than Shape 2
D. Shape 2 has 4 more sides than Shape 1

2.G.1

4. Three shapes are shown.

Shape 1   Shape 2   Shape 3

Which shows the correct order of the Shapes from least number of sides to greatest number of sides?

A. Shape1, Shape 2, Shape 3
B. Shape 3, Shape 1, Shape 2
C. Shape 2, Shape 1, Shape 3
D. Shape 2, Shape 2, Shape 1

2.G.1

5. Three shapes are shown.

Shape 1   Shape 2   Shape 3

Which statement is true?

A. All three shapes have the same number of sides.
B. Shapes 1 and 2 have the same number of sides.
C. Shapes 1 and 3 have the same number of sides.
D. Shapes 2 and 3 have the same number of sides.

2.G.1

TIP of the DAY

Read the questions carefully if you need to add or subtract. Write down the numbers then add or subtract.

WEEK 18 : DAY 5

1. A shape is shown.

Which shows the number of sides?

A. 3
B. 4
C. 5
D. 6

2.G.1

2. Which shape does not have all straight sides?

A.

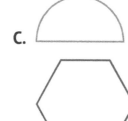

C.

B.

D.

2.G.1

3. Two shapes are shown.

Shape 1   Shape 2

Which shows the total number of sides for Shape 1 and Shape 2?

A. 4
B. 6
C. 7
D. 8

2.G.1

4. Three shapes are shown.

Which shows the total number of sides for all three shapes?

A. 9
B. 12
C. 15
D. 18

2.G.1

DAY 6
Challenge question

How many total sides are there for a 3, 4, 5 and 6 sided shape?

WEEK 19

VIDEO EXPLANATIONS

ARGOPREP.COM

This week we are counting squares and finding equal parts of a shape. We will use addition to find the total number of squares.

You can find detailed video explanations of each problem in the book by visiting:
ArgoPrep.com

WEEK 19 : DAY 1

1. Which shows the total number of squares?

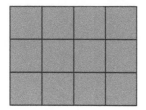

A. 4
B. 7
C. 12
D. 16

2.G.2

2. Which shows the total number of squares?

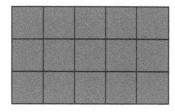

A. 5   C. 15
B. 8   D. 18

2.G.2

3. Which does NOT have a total of 24 squares?

A.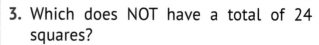

B.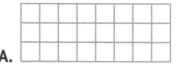

C.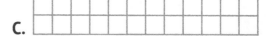

D.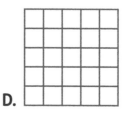

2.G.2

4. Which shows the total number of squares?

A. 11
B. 21
C. 24
D. 28

2.G.2

Rectangles can be made up of equal sized squares. The squares going across are called rows. The squares going up and down are called columns.

TIP
of the
DAY

There are 6 columns

There are 3 rows

3 rows of 6 columns
6 + 6 + 6 = 18 total squares

126

WEEK 19 : DAY 2

1. Which number sentences can be used to find the total number of squares by adding the rows or the columns?

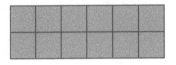

- **A.** 6 + 6 or 2 + 2 + 2 + 2 + 2 +2
- **B.** 2 + 2 or 6 + 6 + 6 + 6 + 6 + 6
- **C.** 6 + 2 + 2 or 2 + 2 + 2 + 2 + 2 + 2
- **D.** 6 + 2 or 6 + 2 + 6 + 2 + 6 + 2

2.G.2

2. Which shows the total number of squares?

- **A.** 4
- **B.** 8
- **C.** 12
- **D.** 16

2.G.2

3. Which shows the total number of squares?

- **A.** 16
- **B.** 30
- **C.** 54
- **D.** 60

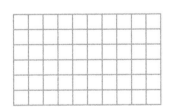

2.G.2

4. Which statement is true about the shape shown?

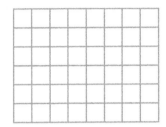

- **A.** There are 6 rows of 6 squares
- **B.** There are 6 rows of 8 squares
- **C.** There are 6 columns of 6 squares
- **D.** There are 8 columns of 8 squares

2.G.2

5. Which shows the total number of squares?

- **A.** 13
- **B.** 15
- **C.** 27
- **D.** 30

2.G.2

TIP of the DAY

To find the total number of squares, you can add the row totals or add the column total.

1. Which shape has equal parts?

A.   C.

B.   D.

2.G.3

3. Which shape is cut into thirds?

A.   C.

B.   D.

2.G.3

2. Which shape is NOT cut into halves?

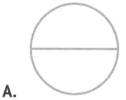

A.   C.

B.   D.

2.G.3

4. Which shape is cut into fourths?

A.   C.

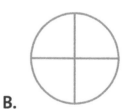 

B.   D.

2.G.3

TIP of the DAY

Shapes can have equal parts. We count the number of equal parts that the shape has. Two equal parts are called halves. Three equal parts are called thirds. Four equal parts are called fourths.

1. A shape is shown.

Which describes the shape?

A. The shape is cut into halves.
B. The shape is cut into thirds.
C. The shape is cut into fourths.
D. The shape is not cut into equal parts.

2.G.3

2. A shape is shown.

Which describes the shape?

A. The shape is cut into halves.
B. The shape is cut into thirds.
C. The shape is cut into fourths.
D. The shape is not cut into equal parts.

2.G.3

3. A shape is shown.

Which describes the shape?

A. The shape is cut into halves.
B. The shape is cut into thirds.
C. The shape is cut into fourths.
D. The shape is not cut into equal parts.

2.G.3

4. A shape is shown.

Which describes the shape?

A. The shape is cut into halves.
B. The shape is cut into thirds.
C. The shape is cut into fourths.
D. The shape is not cut into equal parts.

2.G.3

5. A shape is shown.

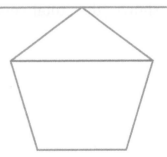

Which describes the shape?

A. The shape is cut into halves.
B. The shape is cut into thirds.
C. The shape is cut into fourths.
D. The shape is not cut into equal parts.

2.G.3

TIP of the DAY

Count the number of equal parts for shapes to describe the parts of the shape.

WEEK 19 : DAY 5

1. Which shows the total number of squares?

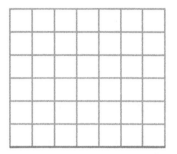

A. 14
B. 36
C. 42
D. 49

2.G.2

2. Which shows the total number of squares?

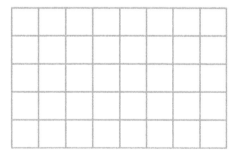

A. 24
B. 36
C. 40
D. 45

2.G.2

3. Which shape is NOT cut into fourths?

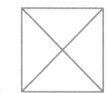

A.

C.

B.

D.

2.G.3

4. A shape is shown.

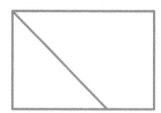

Which describes the shape?

A. The shape is cut into halves.
B. The shape is cut into thirds.
C. The shape is cut into fourths.
D. The shape is not cut into equal parts.

2.G.3

DAY 6
Challenge question

A shape is cut into 3 equal parts. What do we call each part?

130

WEEK 20

VIDEO EXPLANATIONS ▶ ARGOPREP.COM

This week we are reviewing what we know from weeks 11-19. You can review weeks 11-19 to make sure you remember all of the skills.

You can find detailed video explanations of each problem in the book by visiting:
ArgoPrep.com

1. Which shows the length of the crayon?

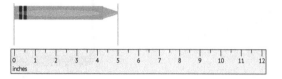

A. 5 inches
C. 5 centimeters
B. 6 inches
D. 6 centimeters

2.MD.1

2. Which shows the length of the fish?

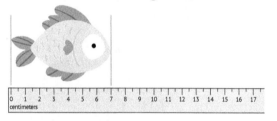

A. 7 inches
C. 7 centimeters
B. 8 inches
D. 8 centimeters

2.MD.1

3. Which could show the length of a couch?

A. 7 feet
B. 7 inches
C. 7 meters
D. 7 centimeters

2.MD.3

4. The pin has a length of 1 inch.

Which shows the length of the bookmark?

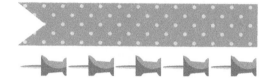

A. 5 inches
C. 5 centimeters
B. 6 inches
D. 6 centimeters

2.MD.2

5. The lengths of a glue stick and a toothbrush are shown.

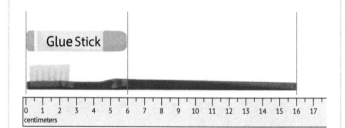

Which shows how much longer the toothbrush is than the glue stick?

A. 6 centimeters
B. 10 centimeters
C. 16 centimeters
D. 22 centimeters

2.MD.4

TIP of the DAY

When doing different kinds of problems, take time to remember similar problems that you did before.

1. The length of a window is 3 feet. The length of the wall next to the window is 13 feet. Which shows the total length of the window and the wall?

   A. 3 feet
   B. 10 feet
   C. 13 feet
   D. 16 feet

   2.MD.5

2. The height of desk is 28 inches. A boy is 15 inches taller than the desk. Which shows the height of the boy?

   A. 13 inches
   B. 15 inches
   C. 28 inches
   D. 43 inches

   2.MD.5

3. A number line is shown.

   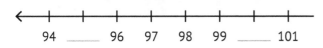

   | | | | | | | | |
   |94| |96|97|98|99| |101|

   Which shows the missing pair of numbers?

   A. 93 and 98
   B. 95 and 98
   C. 93 and 100
   D. 95 and 100

   2.MD.6

4. A number chart is shown.

37	38	39	40
?	48	49	50
57	58	59	?

   Which two number complete the chart?

   A. 47 and 58
   B. 49 and 58
   C. 47 and 60
   D. 49 and 60

   2.MD.6

5. A number chart is shown.

28	30	?	34	?	38

   Which pair of numbers completes the chart?

   A. 31 and 35
   B. 31 and 36
   C. 32 and 35
   D. 32 and 36

   2.MD.6

TIP of the DAY

A number line can be very helpful so we can visually see what happens when we add or subtract numbers. In the future, number lines will help you understand positive and negative numbers.

WEEK 20 : DAY 3

1. Which shows the time on the clock?

A. 4:06　　　C. 5:06
B. 4:30　　　D. 5:30

2.MD.7

2. Which shows the time on the clock?

A. 9 minutes to 6
B. 15 minutes to 6
C. 9 minutes after 5
D. 15 minutes after 6

2.MD.7

3. Which shows the amount of money equal to 3 dollars, 3 dimes, 3 nickels and 3 pennies?

A. $3.33　　　C. $3.48
B. $3.43　　　D. $3.98

2.MD.8

4. Which shows the amount of money equal to 88 cents using the least number of coins?

A. 3 quarters 1 dime and 3 pennies
B. 3 quarters 1 nickel and 8 pennies
C. 3 quarters 2 nickels and 3 pennies
D. 2 quarters 2 dimes 2 nickels and 8 pennies

2.MD.8

5. Which shows the total amount of money?

A. $4.16
B. $4.21
C. $4.31
D. $4.76

2.MD.8

TIP of the DAY

Try this challenge problem!
It's a quarter past three. What time is it?

134

Use the bar graph below for questions 1-5.
The bar graph shows the number of pictures painted by students in grades 1-4 in art class.

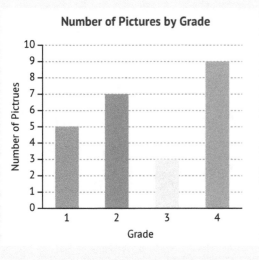

Number of Pictures by Grade

3. Which grade had the most pictures?

A. 1
B. 2
C. 3
D. 4

2.MD.10

4. Which shows how many more pictures were from Grade 2 than from Grade 3?

A. 3
B. 4
C. 7
D. 11

2.MD.10

1. Which shows the number of pictures from Grade 2 students?

A. 3   C. 7
B. 5   D. 9

2.MD.10

5. Which shows the total amount of pictures?

A. 10
B. 14
C. 15
D. 24

2.MD.10

2. Which grade has 5 pictures?

A. 1
B. 2
C. 3
D. 4

2.MD.10

TIP
of the
DAY

Try this challenge problem!
It's a quarter to five. What time is it?

135

1. Which shows the total number of squares?

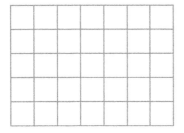

A. 20
B. 28
C. 35
D. 42

2.G.2

3. Which shape is cut into equal parts?

A.

C.

B.

D.

2.G.3

2. Which shape does NOT have 4 sides?

A.

C.

B.

D.

2.G.1

4. Which shape is cut into thirds?

A.

C.

B.

D.

2.G.3

DAY 6
Challenge question

Cut the shape into fourths.

136

THE
END

**Great job finishing all 20 weeks!
You should be ready for any test.**

ASSESSMENT

Try this assessment to see how much you've learned - good luck!

1. There were 6 oranges in a box. Then 7 more oranges were put in the box. Which shows the total number of oranges?

   A. 12
   B. 13
   C. 14
   D. 15

   2.OA.2

2. Ray had 15 pencils. He gave 6 to some friends. Which shows the number of pencils that Ray has left?

   A. 8
   B. 9
   C. 11
   D. 21

   2.OA.2

3. Which number completes the number sentence?

   $$8 + 6 = 10 + ?$$

   A. 2
   B. 4
   C. 6
   D. 14

   2.OA.2

4. Which number sentence has a sum that is even?

   A. $5 + 2 = ?$
   B. $5 + 4 = ?$
   C. $5 + 5 = ?$
   D. $5 + 6 = ?$

   2.OA.3

5. Last week there were 75 toy cars in a store. Then 26 were sold.

   Which shows the number of toy cars now in the store?

   A. 41
   B. 49
   C. 51
   D. 59

   2.NBT.5

6. The teacher had 55 folders last week. Today the teacher brought in 19 more. Which shows the total number of folders?

   A. 36
   B. 46
   C. 64
   D. 74

   2.NBT.5

ASSESSMENT

7. Which number sentence is shown using the model?

- A. 4 + 4 = ?
- B. 4 + 5 = ?
- C. 4 + 4 + 4 + 4 + 4 = ?
- D. 4 + 5 + 4 + 5 + 4 = ?

2.OA.4

8. Which number has 7 tens, 2 ones and 1 hundred?

- A. 127
- B. 172
- C. 712
- D. 721

2.NBT.1

9. Which shows the number five hundred eight?

- A. 58
- B. 85
- C. 508
- D. 580

2.NBT.3

10. Which symbol completes the number sentence?

Seven hundred seventy six ? 767

- A. <
- B. >
- C. =

2.NBT.4

11. Which set of numbers starts at 315 and skip counts by 10?

- A. 315, 316, 317, 318
- B. 315, 320, 325, 330,
- C. 315, 325, 335, 345
- D. 315, 415, 515, 615

2.NBT.8

12. Which number completes the number sentence?

$$27 + ? = 57$$

- A. 3
- B. 20
- C. 30
- D. 84

2.NBT.5

13. Which shows the sum of 36 + 3 + 18?

    A. 47

    B. 57

    C. 74

    D. 84

2.NBT.6

14. Which number is 10 more than 235?

    A. 135

    B. 225

    C. 245

    D. 345

2.NBT.8

Use the model below for questions 15-16.

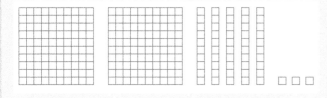

15. Which shows the sum of the number in the model and 178?

    A. 75

    B. 175

    C. 321

    D. 431

2.NBT.7

16. Which shows the difference of the number in the model and 178?

    A. 75   **C.** 321

    B. 175   **D.** 431

2.NBT.7

Use the figure below for questions 17-19.
The lengths of a crayon and pencil are shown.

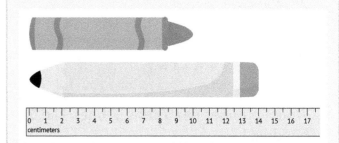

17. Which statement is true about the lengths?

    A. The length of the crayon is 10 inches and the length of the pencil is 14 inches.

    B. The length of the crayon is 14 inches and the length of the pencil is 10 inches.

    C. The length of the crayon is 10 centimeters and the length of the pencil is 14 centimeters.

    D. The length of the crayon is 14 centimeters and the length of the pencil is 10 centimeters.

2.MD.4

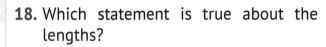
18. Which statement is true about the lengths?

    A. The length of the crayon is 4 inches greater than the length of the pencil.

    B. The length of the pencil is 4 inches greater than the length of the crayon.

    C. The length of the crayon is 4 centimeters greater than the length of the pencil.

    D. The length of the pencil is 4 centimeters greater than the length of the crayon.

2.MD.4

19. Which shows the sum of the two lengths?

    A. 4

    B. 10

    C. 14

    D. 24

2.MD.5

20. Which could be the length of a soccer field?

    A. 110 inches

    B. 110 meters

    C. 110 centimeters

2.MD.3

21. The length of a toy animal is 15 inches. The length of toy truck is 3 inches longer.

Which shows the length of the toy truck?

    A. 3 inches

    B. 12 inches

    C. 15 inches

    D. 18 inches

2.MD.5

22. A number chart is shown.

27	28	29
?	38	39
47	?	49

Which pair of numbers completes the chart?

    A. 30 and 46

    B. 30 and 48

    C. 37 and 46

    D. 37 and 48

2.MD.6

23. Which shows the time on the clock?

    A. 12:06   **C.** 1:06

    B. 12:30   **D.** 1:30

2.MD.7

24. Which shows the total amount of money?

A. $3.32	**C.** $3.62
B. $3.42	**D.** $3.72

2.MD.8

25. Which shows the amount of $1.19 using the least number of coins?

A. 3 quarters 4 dimes 4 pennies
B. 3 quarters 3 dimes 14 pennies
C. 4 quarters 3 nickels 4 pennies
D. 4 quarters 1 dime 1 nickel 4 pennies

2.MD.8

Use the pictograph below for questions 26-27.

Dog Sizes	
Small Dogs	🐾🐾🐾🐾🐾
Medium Dogs	🐾🐾
Large Dogs	🐾🐾🐾

Key: 🐾 = 1 Dog

26. The students that had dogs were asked to tell if their dog was small, medium, or large sized. The pictograph shows the number of dogs for each size.

Which number shows how many more small dogs than medium dogs?

A. 2	**C.** 5
B. 3	**D.** 7

2.MD.10

27. Which shows the total number of dogs?

A. 7
B. 8
C. 9
D. 10

2.MD.10

28. Which does NOT have a total of 12 squares?

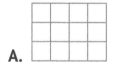
A.

C.

B.

D.

2.G.2

29. Which shape does not have 6 straight sides?

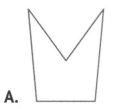

A.

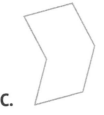

C.

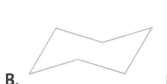

B.

D.

2.G.1

30. Which shape is NOT cut into fourths?

A.

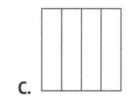

C.

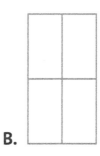

B.

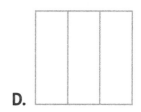

D.

2.G.3

ARGOPREP.COM

VIDEO
EXPLANATIONS ▶

ANSWER KEY

WEEK 1

DAY 1	DAY 2	DAY 3	DAY 4	DAY 5
1. B	1. C	1. C	1. D	1. B
2. C	2. D	2. D	2. B	2. C
3. B	3. A	3. C	3. C	3. A
4. A	4. D	4. D	4. C	4. D
5. C	5. B	5. A	5. D	5. A
	6. A		6. C	6. D

WEEK 2

DAY 1	DAY 2	DAY 3	DAY 4	DAY 5
1. D	1. A	1. D	1. C	1. B
2. C	2. C	2. B	2. D	2. B
3. A	3. D	3. C	3. C	3. B
4. A	4. A	4. A	4. D	4. D
5. B	5. C	5. A	5. C	5. D
			6. A	6. B

WEEK 3

DAY 1	DAY 2	DAY 3	DAY 4	DAY 5
1. B	1. C	1. D	1. B	1. C
2. C	2. B	2. B	2. C	2. B
3. B	3. A	3. C	3. A	3. A
4. D	4. B	4. A	4. C	4. D
5. C	5. C	5. B	5. B	5. B
6. A	6. B	6. D	6. D	6. B

WEEK 4

DAY 1	DAY 2	DAY 3	DAY 4	DAY 5
1. A	1. B	1. B	1. D	1. C
2. B	2. C	2. C	2. D	2. A
3. D	3. D	3. B	3. C	3. D
4. B	4. A	4. A	4. A	4. B
5. A	5. B	5. D	5. B	5. B
6. C	6. D	6. C		

WEEK 5

DAY 1	DAY 2	DAY 3	DAY 4	DAY 5
1. B	1. C	1. C	1. B	1. B
2. D	2. B	2. B	2. C	2. B
3. C	3. A	3. C	3. A	3. D
4. A	4. C	4. A	4. B	4. C
5. A	5. D	5. D	5. C	5. B
6. C	6. A			6. D

WEEK 6

DAY 1	DAY 2	DAY 3	DAY 4	DAY 5
1. D	1. C	1. D	1. B	1. B
2. B	2. D	2. D	2. B	2. B
3. D	3. B	3. D	3. B	3. D
4. C	4. B	4. C	4. A	4. A
5. B	5. D	5. C	5. A	5. A
6. B	6. D	6. C	6. B	6. D

WEEK 7

DAY 1	DAY 2	DAY 3	DAY 4	DAY 5
1. D	1. C	1. D	1. D	1. B
2. B	2. D	2. D	2. B	2. A
3. C	3. D	3. B	3. C	3. B
4. C	4. C	4. A	4. A	4. D
5. D	5. B	5. D	5. C	5. B
6. D	6. D		6. B	6. C

WEEK 8

DAY 1	DAY 2	DAY 3	DAY 4	DAY 5
1. C	1. D	1. B	1. D	1. B
2. C	2. C	2. B	2. A	2. D
3. C	3. B	3. A	3. A	3. B
4. A	4. D	4. A	4. B	4. C
5. A	5. C	5. B	5. D	5. B
6. D			6. C	6. C

ANSWER KEY

WEEK 9

DAY 1	DAY 2	DAY 3	DAY 4	DAY 5
1. A	1. A	1. C	1. B	1. A
2. D	2. B	2. D	2. A	2. A
3. B	3. B	3. C	3. D	3. C
4. A	4. C	4. A	4. B	4. A
5. A	5. D	5. A	5. B	5. B
6. D	6. D	6. A	6. B	6. A

WEEK 10

DAY 1	DAY 2	DAY 3	DAY 4	DAY 5
1. C	1. D	1. D	1. D	1. C
2. D	2. B	2. A	2. A	2. C
3. D	3. C	3. D	3. C	3. D
4. C	4. A	4. C	4. D	4. B
5. A	5. D	5. B	5. C	5. A
6. B	6. A	6. D	6. C	6. A

WEEK 11

DAY 1	DAY 2	DAY 3	DAY 4	DAY 5
1. D	1. A	1. A	1. B	1. C
2. B	2. D	2. B	2. A	2. B
3. D	3. C	3. A	3. C	3. A
4. D	4. A	4. D	4. A	4. A
5. A	5. D		5. B	5. B
			6. A	

WEEK 12

DAY 1	DAY 2	DAY 3	DAY 4	DAY 5
1. D	1. B	1. D	1. C	1. C
2. D	2. C	2. C	2. A	2. D
3. A	3. A	3. A	3. C	3. B
4. B	4. C	4. D	4. D	4. D
5. D	5. B	5. A	5. B	5. B
6. A	6. C	6. B	6. D	6. C

WEEK 13

DAY 1	DAY 2	DAY 3	DAY 4	DAY 5
1. B	1. D	1. C	1. C	1. A
2. B	2. A	2. D	2. A	2. C
3. C	3. C	3. C	3. D	3. D
4. C	4. C	4. B	4. D	4. C
5. A	5. B	5. D	5. D	5. A

WEEK 14

DAY 1	DAY 2	DAY 3	DAY 4	DAY 5
1. A	1. D	1. B	1. A	1. B
2. B	2. D	2. B	2. B	2. B
3. D	3. D	3. C	3. D	3. D
4. D	4. D	4. A	4. B	4. D
5. D	5. B	5. C	5. B	5. C
			6. D	

WEEK 15

DAY 1	DAY 2	DAY 3	DAY 4	DAY 5
1. B	1. B	1. D	1. C	1. D
2. C	2. C	2. C	2. D	2. C
3. D	3. A	3. C	3. C	3. B
4. D	4. D	4. B	4. A	4. C
5. C	5. B	5. C	5. B	5. D
6. C	6. C			

WEEK 16

DAY 1	DAY 2	DAY 3	DAY 4	DAY 5
1. B	1. C	1. A	1. B	1. B
2. B	2. D	2. C	2. A	2. B
3. B	3. C	3. B	3. C	3. A
4. C	4. D	4. C	4. B	4. B
5. A	5. B	5. D	5. B	5. C

ANSWER KEY

WEEK 17

DAY 1	DAY 2	DAY 3	DAY 4	DAY 5
1. A	1. D	1. A	1. A	1. C
2. B	2. A	2. D	2. B	2. C
3. B	3. D	3. C	3. D	3. C
4. C	4. D	4. C	4. C	4. A
5. C	5. A	5. B	5. A	5. D

WEEK 18

DAY 1	DAY 2	DAY 3	DAY 4	DAY 5
1. B	1. C	1. B	1. C	1. B
2. C	2. B	2. C	2. B	2. C
3. C	3. B	3. A	3. A	3. D
4. B	4. B	4. D	4. C	4. C
	5. D		5. D	

WEEK 19

DAY 1	DAY 2	DAY 3	DAY 4	DAY 5
1. C	1. A	1. D	1. B	1. C
2. C	2. D	2. C	2. D	2. C
3. D	3. D	3. A	3. C	3. B
4. D	4. B	4. B	4. A	4. D
	5. D		5. D	

WEEK 20

DAY 1	DAY 2	DAY 3	DAY 4	DAY 5
1. A	1. D	1. B	1. C	1. C
2. C	2. D	2. B	2. A	2. D
3. A	3. D	3. C	3. D	3. C
4. A	4. C	4. A	4. B	4. D
5. B	5. D	5. A	5. D	

Challenge Question

Week 1: Standard form - 270. Written form- two hundred seventy. Expanded form - 200 + 70

Week 2: 300 + 120 + 12 = 432, 432 > 322

Week 3: 5 + 9 = 14, 6 + 8 = 14, 7 + 7 = 14. Notice that as one number increases the other decreases and there are two 7's together

Week 4: 8 + 7 = 15 8 – 7 = 1. Sum of 15, difference of 1

Week 5: Odd + Even possible examples. 3 + 2 = 5, 5 + 4 = 9, 7 + 6 = 13. Odd + Even = Odd because the even makes a pair, adding an odd will result in 1 extra.

Week 6: 40 + 35 = 75 (Any pair of numbers that equal 75 when added)

40 – 35 = 5 (Same pair of numbers subtracted)

Week 7: 53 + 100 = 153; 153 + 10 = 163; 163 + 100 = 263 cans in all

Week 8: 555

Week 9: A. 80

B. 40 + 40 = 80 (Any pair of numbers that equal 80 when added).

Week 11: 6 crayons will equal 36 inches. Add 6 + 6 = 12. Every 2 crayons = 12 inches. 3 set of 2 crayons = 12 + 12 +

+ 12 = 36 inches

Week 12: One side = 5 cm. There are 4 sides-5+5+5+5 = = 20 cm.

Week 13: 22 cm. 3+3+3+3 = 12 cm. 22 + 12 = 34 cm.

Week 14:

Week 15: 88 cents in 9 coins

2 quarters (50 cents) 3 dimes (30 cents) 1 nickel (5 cents) 3 pennies (3 cents)

amount of money: 50 + 30 + 5 + 3 = 88 cents

number of coins: 2 + 3 + 1 + 3 = 9

Week 16:

Week 17: Any question for the bar graph.

Week 18: 18

Week 19: Thirds

Week 20: Shape cut into fourths

ANSWER KEY

Middle Assessment

1. B	12. C	23. C
2. A	13. A	24. B
3. A	14. C	25. D
4. C	15. D	26. D
5. D	16. C	27. D
6. C	17. B	28. C
7. B	18. C	29. D
8. C	19. A	30. D
9. B	20. B	
10. D	21. C	
11. C	22. B	

End of Year Assessment

1. B	12. C	23. B
2. B	13. B	24. C
3. B	14. C	25. D
4. C	15. D	26. B
5. B	16. A	27. D
6. D	17. C	28. B
7. C	18. D	29. A
8. B	19. D	30. D
9. C	20. B	
10. B	21. D	
11. C	22. D	

COMMON CORE TEST SERIES

The goal of these workbooks is to provide mock state tests so students can increase confidence and test scores during actual test day.

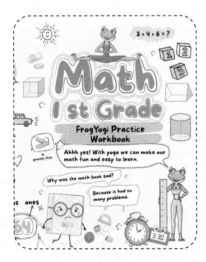

FrogYogi Math Series

It combines fun and engaging activities along with math concepts. Your child will be hooked in learning math on a daily basis. This workbook includes fun and effective yoga math breaks between solving problems helping the brain relax and retain more information.

KIDS WINTER ACADEMY

Kids Winter Academy by ArgoPrep covers material learned in September through December so your child can reinforce the concepts they should have learned in class. We recommend using this particular series during the winter break. This workbook includes two weeks of activities for math, reading, science, and social studies. Best of all, you can access detailed video explanations to all the questions on our website.

Award-Winning Program

500,000+ students, teachers and parents use ArgoPrep. Join the family!

**Mom's Choice
Gold Award**

**Homeschool Seal
of Approval**

**Parents's Choice
Gold Award**

**Education Hero
of The Year**

**National Parenting
Product Award**

**Tillywig Brain
Child Award**

**The EdTech Cool
Tool Award**

**The EdTech
Leadership Award**

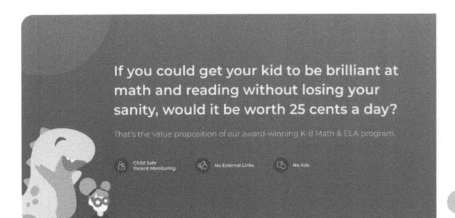

If you could get your kid to be brilliant at math and reading without losing your sanity, would it be worth 25 cents a day?

That's the value proposition of our award-winning K-8 Math & ELA program.

Child Safe Parent Monitoring   No External Links   No Ads

Premium

FREE 9.99$ SAVE 100%

- ✓ 30,000+ Practice Questions
- ✓ 500+ Video Lectures
- ✓ 15,000+ Video Explanations
- ✓ Printable Worksheets
- ✓ 14 Days Free Trial
- ✓ One subscription for all your kids
- ✓ Progress Reporting

VISIT ARGOPREP.COM/K8

Take a look inside!

Your Child Moves Ahead of the Class With ArgoPrep

K-8 Math and ELA Video Lectures

Your subscription includes ALL grades so you can access video lessons from different grades. We cover and teach every topic your child needs to know for their grade level! All of our video lessons are taught by licensed-teachers and the videos are designed to be engaging!

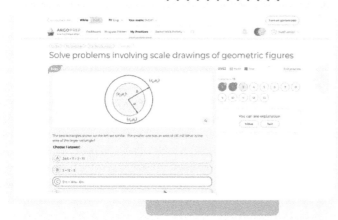

Gap-Proofing Quizzes

Our quizzes gauge student mastery level of any particular topic. If your child struggles, each quiz question has an explanation video to accompany it, so students don't fall through those "learning gaps". If they need more information, they can always review last year's videos and worksheets as well.

Unlimited Printable Worksheets

Print your worksheets from our database of thousands! We are constantly creating new, educator-approved worksheets for grades K-8 in our ever-expanding resource collection! Our worksheets are unique because we include fewer questions and more visually balanced spaces. Our amazing illustrations are 100% kid-approved!

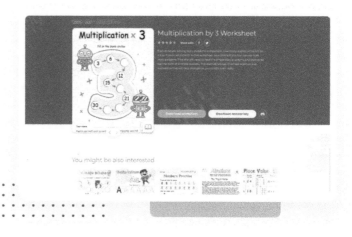

CPSIA information can be obtained
at www.ICGtesting.com
Printed in the USA
BVHW081323121121
621448BV00012BA/527

9 781951 048662